A People in Focus Book

Madam Prime Minister

A Biography of Margaret Thatcher

LIBBY HUGHES

ᕹ|DILLON PRESS, INC.
Minneapolis, Minnesota 55415

Acknowledgments

I would like to thank the following people for their cooperation: From Grantham—Jill Harrison, Mrs. Mair Thomas, Mrs. Gladys Foster, Eric and Margaret Tuckwood, Mrs. Hazel Packham, Mrs. Noreen Miller, Mr. and Mrs. Hugh Brammer, Miss Nellie Towers, John Hay, Peter Dean, Andrew Plaice, John Pinchbeck, and Jim Allen, town historian; Shirley Whitton and Janet Stanton at Kesteven; Mrs. Barrow, Dartford Conservative office; Margaret Phillimore; Raymond Woollcott of Dartford; Finchley Advertiser; Oxford Mail; Denis Kendall of Los Angeles; Michael Bates and Terry J. Perks of 10 Downing Street's Press Office; Sir Nicholas Bonsor, House of Commons; Isabel Ratcliffe and Michael Price, British Embassy in Washington, D.C.; Elizabeth Kerr, Camera Press of London; Liz Moore, Popperfoto of London; Tom Schneider and Lisa Erskine at Dillon Press; and Lucy Post Frisbee.

Photographs have been reproduced through the courtesy of the United Nations; the British Embassy, Washington, D.C.; S. Dukanovic, S. Ferguson, D. O'Neill, R. Slade, I. Swift, and L. Wilson/Camera Press—Globe Photos; Somerville College, Oxford University; Popperfoto; UPI/Bettman News-photos; and the U.S. National Archives, Office of Presidential Libraries. Cover photo by Norman Parkinson, Camera Press—Globe Photos.

Library of Congress Cataloging-in-Publication Data

Hughes, Libby.
    Madam Prime Minister : a biography of Margaret Thatcher / by Libby Hughes.
        p.   cm. (A People in focus book)
    Bibliography: p.
    Includes index.
    Summary: Examines the childhood, education, and political career of the woman who has been elected prime minister of Great Britain three times.
    ISBN 0-87518-410-3
    1. Thatcher, Margaret—Juvenile literature. 2. Prime minis-ters—Great Britain—Biography—Juvenile literature. 3. Great Britain—Politics and government—1979—Juvenile literature. [1. Thatcher, Margaret. 2. Prime ministers.] I. Title. II. Series.
DA591.T47H84   1989
941.085'8'092—dc20
[B]
[92]   89-11974
                                                            CIP
                                                            AC

Dillon Press, Inc., 242 Portland Avenue South
Minneapolis, Minnesota 55415

Printed in the United States of America
    2 3 4 5 6 7 8 9 10 98 97 96 95 94 93 92 91 90

Contents

Chapter/One

A Drive to Win

The eleven-year-old girl didn't know what real fear was or how it felt. She only knew that she had memorized her piece for this speech contest, and now it was time to say it before the town audience at the Finkin Street Methodist Church where the second *eisteddford* (a competition in music and the arts) was being held in her home town of Grantham, England, in February 1937.

The hum and chatter of the audience stopped when her name was called. She marched forward and, for one so young, spoke clearly and in measured tones. After she finished, the audience clapped loudly. She then entered a piano solo, and a piano duet with her friend, Eileen Jubb. When all the performers had finished and the winner's name was read, the round-faced little girl with the pink cheeks walked forward again, this time to receive her prize—a silver medal in the junior speech class, and a gold medal for her piano duet. Her parents and sister smiled broadly, clapping harder than all the rest.

Afterwards, a teacher from her school went over to shake her hand and tell her how lucky she was to win. The eleven-year-old girl stiffened her back, stared directly at the teacher, and told her she wasn't lucky: "I deserved it," she replied.

That forthright young girl was Margaret Hilda Roberts before her name became Margaret Thatcher by marriage.

Winning, winning, winning—this would be the pattern of Margaret Roberts's life from the time she was born on October 13, 1925, in Grantham, England, to her years as prime minister. Although success and prizes appeared to come easily, Margaret Roberts worked hard to get what she wanted. Winning was the reward.

Almost forty years after that first speech prize, she was to win another victory. This time the stage was a political race fought against Edward Heath, and the prize was to be the leadership of the British Conservative (Tory) party. She defeated Heath and became the party's first woman leader.

The reporters gathered around her, shouting dozens of questions. When one of them asked why she thought she had won, she said simply, "Merit."

By the time she won the prime ministership of Great Britain for the third time in 1987, the reporters didn't have to ask that question again. They knew what her answer would be: "Merit."

Where did this drive to win come from?

The greatest influence in Margaret's life was her father. Alfred Roberts was the kind of man you wouldn't forget, and Margaret adored him. He was very tall—six feet, three inches. His spectacles were thick and horn-rimmed, and a shock of blonde hair fell over his forehead and turned white as he grew older.

Alf Roberts had to leave school at the age of thirteen to help support his own parents and their seven children. Because his eyesight was too poor to go into his father's shoemaking business, he had to find another occupation. Secretly, he wanted to become a teacher, but without a full education, that wasn't possible, and his father couldn't afford to pay for Alfred's schooling.

Instead, Alf took a job in a local grocer's store where he did everything from sweeping floors and running errands to handling money and ordering goods. At the end of every week, he handed his

money over to his mother and father until he became an adult. Then, he moved forty miles away
from his hometown to Grantham, where he
worked as an assistant manager in a grocer's shop.

Not long after this, he met his bride-to-be, Beatrice Stephenson, a young dressmaker who made
children's clothes and wedding dresses in her parents' house. Beatrice was a quiet, shy woman.
After she and Alfred were married, her role and
influence in the family were not as strong as her
husband's, except in music. She made clothes for
the girls, cleaned the home, worked in the shop,
and supported her husband in whatever he did.

Alfred Roberts, on the other hand, usually
made his presence known. When Alfred was angry, his friends and family knew it. To his daughters, he seemed taller than the Tower of London.
He only had to glare at them through those magni-
fied lenses from under that mop of white hair, and,
without saying a word, they did whatever he insisted they do.

Alfred and Beatrice Roberts both worked hard
to save enough money for Alfred to buy his own
grocer's shop. Financially, they could only afford
a store in the poorer section of Grantham on
North Parade Street. But it was a beginning, and it
was all theirs.

Chapter/Two

Sacrificing Popularity

Grantham, England, where the sun is called a yellowbelly and the moon a fireball, lies 100 miles north of London in Lincolnshire. Saint Wulfram's church spire, the third largest in England, can be seen silhouetted against Grantham's skies for miles. With a population of 25,000 or more, the city was the crossroads for horse and buggy traffic in the days before the invention of cars or trains.

King John and his traveling companions stayed at Grantham's Angel and Royal Inn around the year 1213. Charles Dickens once lodged in the George Hotel, and in his novel *Nicholas Nickleby* called it the finest inn anywhere. Mathematician Isaac Newton (1642-1727), who discovered the law of gravity, went to the King's School for boys

Saint Wulfram's church spire towers over the buildings of Grantham, England.

there and carved his name on the stone ledge of one of the school windows.

Full of old world charm, Grantham was an agricultural village known for its tasty beef and sausages. During World War II, that slow pace changed. Outside the town was the British Manufacture and Research Company, the most bombed factory in Britain. The company's 8,000 workers made guns, shells, barrels, and cannons for the Spitfire, Hurrican, and Mosquito fighter planes. The nearby headquarters of the British Bomber Command was also a target for German bombing raids.

Born in the apartment above her parents' grocery shop, Margaret Roberts and her sister, Muriel, who was four years older, grew up in the rural quiet of Grantham until their lives were interrupted by World War II.

The family's small apartment was furnished with heavy, secondhand furniture, but it was always neat and clean. Without indoor hot running water, Mrs. Roberts filled Victorian jugs and basins that sat on each bedroom bureau for washing faces and hands, and brushing teeth. The toilet was outside at the bottom of the garden, which was not unusual because every apartment and house had the same kind of plumbing. Once a week the family took baths in the grocery warehouse by hauling buckets of hot water from the store across the courtyard to fill a wooden tub.

Margaret's grandmother, Phoebe Crust Stephenson, moved into the family's cramped quarters above the grocery store in the 1920s. She was a lively, outspoken woman, and Margaret enjoyed listening to her wisdom and advice. Her views were very much like those of Alf Roberts regarding Sundays and her "waste not, want not" philosophy. She died nine days before Margaret turned nine years old, which was a sad loss for the family.

Religion played a major part in the lives of the

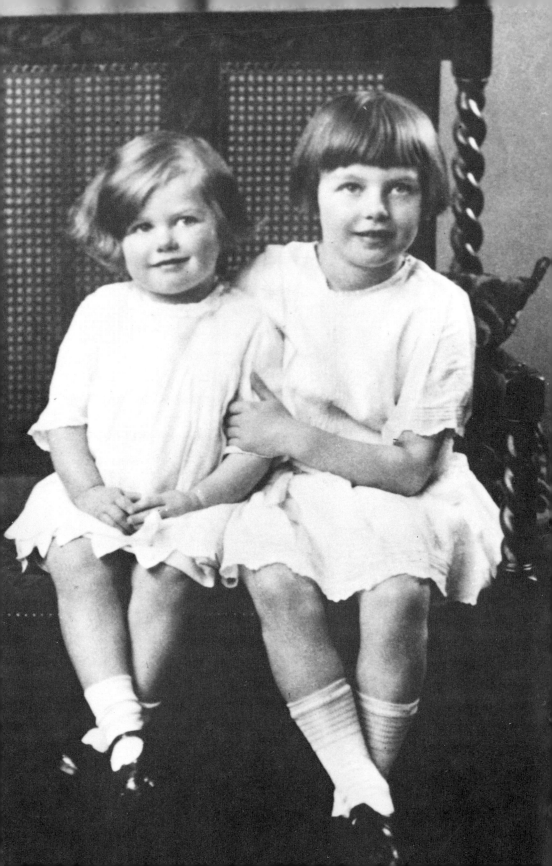

Roberts family. Sundays were busy. Mrs. Roberts was up early to do the baking before walking with the family to the Finkin Street Methodist Church four different times throughout the day. Sunday school was at 10:00 A.M., church at 11:00 A.M., another Sunday school session at 2:30 P.M., and another church service at 6:00 P.M.

Margaret accepted this strict routine without question until she overheard her friends talking about the fun they had on Sundays with their families, going on picnics, playing games, walking, or riding bicycles.

She began to resent Sundays. In fact, she dreaded them. These feelings of resentment grew inside her. Finally, she gathered her courage and dared to face her father. Why couldn't they be like other families and have some fun? Margaret asked. Why couldn't they go to church just once or twice instead of all day?

Mr. Roberts looked calmly at his daughter through his thick glasses. After listening to her outburst, he was silent for what seemed an eternity to the waiting girl. Then he answered her, "Margaret, never do things or want to do things just because other people do them. Make up your own mind about what you are going to do and persuade people to go your way."

The young Margaret Roberts (left) and her older sister, Muriel.

It was her turn to be silent. She thought about what he said and never forgot it. Sundays, from then on, were accepted without moaning or complaining, and without wishing for more fun and free time. Her father's words of advice were to guide her throughout her life, and she would quote them again and again.

"We were Methodist, and Methodist means method," Margaret once commented. "We were taught what was right and wrong in considerable detail. There were certain things you just didn't do and that was that. Duty was very, very strongly ingrained into us."

Miss Nellie Towers, a straight-backed woman with a twinkle in her eye, taught Muriel in Sunday School. "Muriel would bring three-year-old Margaret into class with her. She was precocious [smart for her age] even then and would say the most remarkable things," said Miss Towers. "When she was eleven or twelve, she could play the piano beautifully for the Sunday School. She was mature beyond her years, probably because her father always spoke to her as an adult. She seemed so loyal and sincere. I remember when she took part in a church play as an angel, she sang a solo and insisted on accompanying herself. Somehow she managed it."

As a child, Margaret spent every Sunday in the Finkin Street Methodist Church.

Mr. Roberts's ideas about saving and spending money were as strong as those on religion. Yet he did believe in helping people less fortunate than himself, and taught his daughters to contribute some of their own money to help sick or needy neighbors, rather than depending on the government to take care of them. This kind of welfare, he believed, was more effective.

When they were old enough, Mr. Roberts taught his daughters about the hidden rules for success in England. For centuries, the right family background, the right education, and the right spoken accent have been very important for advancing in society. Regional accents can reflect a certain social class: lower, middle, or upper. Proper accents, like those spoken at such famous boarding schools as Eton and Harrow, or the universities of Oxford and Cambridge, usually express an upper-class background. Although proper diction can be learned, family background cannot be changed. Class differences in England have been unfair to many people over the years, and Mr. Roberts was determined to prepare his girls for overcoming them. He decided his daughters ought to go to a fine school to learn discipline, good manners, and the proper way of speaking.

Since his first store was successful, Mr. Roberts bought a second grocery store on the opposite side of town in order to enroll his daughters in the Huntingtower Road Primary School. He could have sent them to a free national school or to a Church of England school in his own neighborhood, but he selected a county council school more than a mile away, where the girls attended from ages five to ten. As a Methodist, Mr. Roberts did not want the interference that might have come from a Church of England school.

The Huntingtower Road Primary School was a small, red brick building, surrounded by a paved playground. Every morning the children gathered outside on the playground, waiting for the bell to ring to go inside. According to grade and seniority, the students joined their class and marched in single file.

Before and after school, Margaret could run across the street to her father's shop and ask Mrs. Carson, who ran the shop, for a piece of chocolate or a biscuit (an American cookie). Eric Tuckwood, who attended the Huntingtower Road School, remembered Margaret "even at seven years old as very pretty and well turned out, and she often raised her hand to answer questions in the classroom. She was always in the top string [level] of the class."

The Roberts name still appears above the popular Premier Restaurant in Grantham.

Margaret took school very seriously and approached it as she did everything else, determined to learn all she could. Her grades were superior in almost all of her classes. Margaret did not receive these high marks because of pure genius or natural brilliance; she worked two and three hours on homework every night.

After school ended in the afternoon, Margaret and her sister had a cup of tea and biscuits at the store on North Parade and High Street before doing odd jobs for their mother and father. Many of the grocery supplies arrived in large quantities, and the girls were supposed to measure them care-

The original tins and fixtures from the Roberts's store remain on display in the restaurant.

fully and put them in small bags for selling.

"It was quite a big shop. It had a grocery section and a provision section, with all the mahogany fitments that I now see in antique shops, and beautiful canisters of different sorts of tea, coffee, and spices," Margaret recalled in later years. "There was a post office section, confectionary section, and cigarettes. A lot of people came in...and knowing we were all interested in what was going on in the world, we would talk quite late." Today in Grantham, the shop is a restaurant, called the "Premier Restaurant."

The store stayed open late on Fridays and

Saturdays because most people were paid by 5:30 on Friday and did their shopping then. Margaret went to one of the four movie houses in town with her family on Thursday nights, when the shop closed early. This made her very unpopular with her schoolmates, since going to movies on weeknights was not allowed by the school. An exception was made in Margaret's case because she had to work on Friday and Saturday nights.

On Saturdays, Muriel and Margaret Roberts had to help in the store with the crowds of customers. The only exception was sending Margaret to the library on High Street for returning and checking out two books: one for her father, herself, and Muriel, and one for her mother. Mr. Roberts was an avid reader. He read biographies and books about history and politics. He let his wife read novels, but not the girls; they weren't allowed to read anything but nonfiction. Whenever the family was together at dinnertime or during quiet times in the shop, they discussed these books and were encouraged to voice their opinions.

Working in the store was more of a social event than a hardship. Mr. Roberts enjoyed talking about local or national politics with his shoppers. He was elected an alderman (a local representative to a city council) for many years, and he served

Margaret, on the far right, with her mother, Beatrice, her sister, Muriel, and her father, Alfred Roberts, then mayor of Grantham.

one term as mayor of Grantham. Customers liked his company and often stayed at the store to discuss the latest issues. His shop was the local center for information as well as food purchases.

Margaret enjoyed listening to the men exchange ideas or discuss World War II. On September 1, 1939, Germany attacked Poland and then invaded other countries in Europe—the Netherlands, Belgium, France, Yugoslavia, Greece, Norway, and the Soviet Union. Germany's ruler, Adolf Hitler, had established the National Socialist party in the 1920s, better known as the Nazi party, and he wanted to rule most of Europe by force. Alf

Roberts and his friends blamed Hitler for the agony and destruction this war caused.

Mr. Roberts, his friends and customers, and most of the people in Great Britain thought Prime Minister Winston Churchill was right when Great Britain and France declared war on Germany in 1940. From September 7, 1940, through May 10, 1941, German airplanes bombed London every night in a period called the London Blitz. The United States joined the war in December 1941 against Germany and Japan. Through 1944, 190,000 tons of bombs were dropped on Britain, but the spirit of the British people was never broken. Their sense of humor and courage, and Churchill's leadership, carried them through the blackouts, air-raids, and food rationing until the war ended in the summer of 1945.

Mr. Roberts was fascinated by every detail of the war and showed his daughters on a map where all the bombings and landings took place. Partly because of this help from her father, Margaret's knowledge about this subject was somewhat greater than her teachers and classmates. She could explain to them the latest military moves the Germans were making in Great Britain and in other countries.

Because of the war and the long hours in the

two shops, the family had very little free time to-gether. Alf Roberts worked late at his two stores, then ate a hurried supper, and left to attend a variety of local meetings in the community, or to serve as a lay preacher for his church. Often the family did not have dinners or even vacations together. Mrs. Roberts took the girls for a week in summer to the Skegness seaside, not far from Grantham by train, where they stayed in a boarding house. Here, they walked along the high-slung piers, played on the beach, and rode donkeys on the sand.

Mr. Roberts felt he could not leave the store in the hands of anyone but his wife or himself, although he had several assistants. His vacation came later when he took a week alone to play the British game of "bowls." Mr. Roberts liked taking the heavy wooden bowl and rolling it down the long, smooth lawn to hit a target ball at the other end.

Occasionally, the whole family would take a bus to Nottingham on a bank holiday (usually a Monday) to see a movie that might feature Ginger Rogers and Fred Astaire. Going to a pantomime in London during the Christmas holiday season was another favorite thing to do in their spare time.

The British people still love the pantomime, a traditional show performed at Christmastime. A fairytale such as *Jack and the Beanstalk* or *Cinderella* serves as the main theme in the productions. Boys dress as girls and girls as boys. Comic skits, dances, and songs make up a type of variety show within the fairytale. For Margaret, the pantomime and other rare family outings offered a break from her constant school work.

After graduating from Huntingtower, Margaret attended the Kesteven and Grantham Girls' School (high school) in Sandon Road, nearer her home. Each day, she walked from her father's main grocery store, cutting through the narrow back streets to the garden at the Guildhall, where she met several girl friends.

The Kesteven girls were easy to spot in their navy blue tunics, lighter blue blouses, black stockings, and velour hats in winter, or their cotton dresses and straw hats in summer. Overcoats and raincoats were required, but they rarely wore jackets, despite the damp, cold weather. This was a way of developing strong bodies and fresh complexions; to feel the cold was considered a sign of weakness.

Even though Mr. Roberts could afford the cost, he insisted his daughters apply for scholarships based on their grades. Both girls received high grades and partial scholarships to the Kesteven and Granham Girls' School.

Despite her busy schedule, Margaret Roberts did have some fun as a young girl. She played field hockey, became the team's vice-captain, and starred on the debating team. She spent much of her time studying, however, and was considered serious by her classmates, especially when she asked informed, well-phrased questions of visiting lecturers. Later, in a speech as prime minister, she urged other children to follow her example. "If you don't know something," she said, "don't be afraid to ask. It's a sign of intelligence, not ignorance."

As a young teenager, Margaret became aware of herself as a pretty girl. Her sister, Muriel, living and working in Birmingham, England, gave her a powder compact one Christmas. When Margaret powdered her face in school, her friends thought it was a daring and shocking act for someone as perfect as Margaret Roberts.

One of Margaret's friends from the Kesteven school, Noreen Miller, recalled, "When Margaret was asked a question in class and she didn't know the answer, the next day she had all the information. She was very pretty and quite vain about her looks, but we considered she was just one of us. After school, we all went to our own homes. We never visited each other's homes; maybe it was the war. However, I remember Mr. Roberts giving magic lantern shows in his apartment for Margaret's birthday parties. I also remember sitting behind Margaret in school. She used to drive me crazy curling her hair around her finger."

Uniformed and disciplined, Margaret set forth to spend the next six years getting the best education she could. At sixteen, she decided she was ready to go to Oxford University, so she tried to apply at the early age of seventeen.

Chapter / Three

A Non-conformist at Oxford

Margaret wanted to take an exam that would allow her to skip the final year at Kesteven and enroll at Oxford. The idea of staying another entire year at Kesteven made her impatient. She didn't want to do that; wasting time wasn't her style. When Margaret Roberts wanted something, she stubbornly persisted until she got it, and she wanted to be accepted at Somerville College for Women at Oxford University. With all the right qualifications in the sciences—math, chemistry, and biology—nothing seemed to be stopping her.

Margaret's chemistry teacher at Kesteven suggested she apply to Oxford as a chemistry major. Also, Norman Winning, Grantham's town recorder, had majored in physics at Cambridge University and advised Margaret that her chances of being accepted at Oxford were greater in the sciences than in the overcrowded field of the arts and literature.

Margaret was an honors student at Kesteven and felt ready to take the entrance exams and apply to Oxford. Everyone she knew encouraged her to pursue her plan—everyone except the headmistress of Kesteven, Dorothy Gillies. She was a stern and sharply spoken Scotswoman who had replaced the school's founder, Gladys Williams. "We would kill for Miss Williams," said one student. "Miss Gillies ranted and raved."

Until this point, Margaret had always succeeded in persuading people that she was right, but not Gillies. The headmistress blocked Margaret's efforts. Angry and frustrated, Margaret Roberts reportedly faced Gillies and told her, "You're thwarting my ambition."

Dorothy Gillies wouldn't be persuaded, however. There were two problems as she saw it. First, she thought Margaret was too young and would benefit from another year at Kesteven. Second, Margaret needed a certificate in Latin before she could even consider applying at Oxford. This requirement was a real problem because, as a science major, Margaret had not taken any Latin.

"We were not taught Latin in school in those days," remembered Margaret, "so I consulted with my father. He duly reported to me of a conversation he had had with Miss Gillies, and Miss Gillies, apparently, had said to him, 'Your daughter is a very determined young woman, she wants to learn Latin.' And my father turned around and said, 'Miss Gillies, if she says she is going to learn Latin, she is going to learn Latin. So you had better help her.' Well, I did it in ten weeks flat. I did it in the summer recess and I learned then to work all days during the holidays, summer holidays as well as in term time, and we got it."

After being tutored by Victor Wakehouse from the boys' King's School, she was ready. With Latin fresh in her thoughts, she took the entrance exams for Oxford. Chemistry, being her major, was the main focus. Unfortunately, success was not yet to be hers even though she passed everything, including Latin. Her name was placed on a waiting list.

For Margaret, this was a crushing blow. She enrolled once again at Kesteven for what she thought would be another long year. Apparently, Gillies had won the battle. Madeline Edwards (her intellectual rival) and Margaret came back early from summer vacation and were appointed joint head girls. They were both leaders in their own fields of science and the arts and were called "twins" because of the double honor bestowed on them.

Three weeks after the school year started, Margaret received a telegram from Somerville College, offering her a place and a scholarship at Oxford. Her victory over Gillies was a bittersweet one.

With barely three weeks to get ready to leave Grantham and move to the Oxford campus, her father quickly hired two more tutors. One taught her how to play the organ, which Mr. Roberts thought might be useful, and the other gave her speech lessons to make her Lincolnshire accent less noticeable. Since Oxford had only accepted women on a full-time basis since 1920 and was considered an institution for the upper classes, Margaret and her father wanted to make the most of this educational opportunity.

In October 1943, Margaret Roberts arrived at Oxford's Somerville College as a full-time student on scholarship. She loved the small quadrangle, so beautifully lush and green even in December. She felt as if the brick buildings with their Gothic touches seemed to close out the world and protect the female students as they moved freely about the campus.

Somerville College for Women, Oxford University.

But her joy was soon replaced by a severe case of homesickness. This was her first time away from home and family. Her bed/sitting room in the gloomy dark corridors of Penrose Hall had the barest amount of furniture. She felt lonely and depressed.

A friend from Kesteven helped lift her spirits. Margaret Goodrich was a year ahead of her at Oxford, but had shared a biology class with Margaret Roberts back at Kesteven. They had also played on the same hockey team. Canon Goodrich, the minister of a church in a town near Grantham, knew her father and had helped her prepare

for her general Oxford paper. The Goodriches
came to visit Margaret Roberts at Oxford in those
early days at her dormitory, bringing her a box of
freshly baked tea cakes. That show of friendliness
made all the difference for the homesick college
student. Before long, Margaret had settled down
with her classes and had little time to think about
her problems.

The Oxford campus reflected those British pre-
judices that her father had warned her about:
where you lived, where you went to school, and
what your father and grandfather did determined
how you were treated. Of all places, these class
differences were most apparent in the grand eating hall at Somerville College. The arrangement of
tables had social significance. The first set of tables beneath the long table for the principal and professors was for foreign students from wealthy
and well-known families. Indira Gandhi, a former
prime minister of India, had spent her college days
at Somerville and probably ate at these head tables.
The middle tables were for those students on scholarships from the middle class. Finally, the well-
mannered, well-bred, and well-educated students
were seated at the lower tables at the end.

Margaret fit neither with the foreigners nor
with the wealthy group. She was drawn more natu-

The eating hall at Somerville College; Margaret Roberts ate at the middle section of tables.

rally to the tables occupied by the middle class, but never truly felt comfortable with them either. They made fun of her because she talked about her father, her speech lessons, and her accomplishments.

Under the British sytem of university education, based on tutorials and lectures, Margaret was assigned to a tutor, who guided her study and research over three or four years. Her tutor was Professor Dorothy Hodgkin, who later won the Nobel Prize for chemistry in 1964 and the Order of Merit in 1965. With lectures in the morning, laboratory sessions in the afternoons, and some evening lectures, Margaret had a full schedule.

In the 1940s, the majority of university students and professors were liberal in their political thinking. Margaret Roberts, though, was conservative like her father. A Conservative in Great Britain might be compared to a Republican in the United States, and a Labourite to an American Democrat. Margaret's outspoken political ideas made an unforgettable impression on her classmates. Many remembered her for this very fact in future years.

Eventually, she divided her time between chemistry and conservative campus politics, which left little time for making friends. The Oxford Union had produced many famous British politicians, but women were barred from its all-male membership. This, however, did not stop Margaret. She joined the Oxford University Conservative Association (OUCA) and devoted her spare time to that organization. Her only other activity was to sing in the university's Bach choir.

World War II and its nightly air-raids limited social activities for university students. Though dedicated to her studies and restricted by the war, Margaret did find time for a couple of boyfriends. Margaret Goodrich Wickstead recalled, "During the vacations and in later years, Margaret visited us at Corby. By the time of my twenty-first birthday party she had acquired her first boyfriend—some member of the university conservative association to be sure—and he had given her a carnation which had to be kept alive at all costs."

As a young girl in Grantham, Margaret had longed to go to dances and parties on Saturday nights, but she and her sister were not allowed. At Oxford she learned ballroom dancing, which she thoroughly enjoyed.

During her final years at Oxford, she moved into "digs" (shared apartments) with two other girls. Their schedules were so busy that they rarely saw each other, except at breakfast time. In her last year she moved again and had a different set of roommates. To earn money, one summer she taught at the Boys' Central School near Kesteven.

Chemistry seemed to interest her less and less. Her grades were fairly good, and she was working hard, but her spare time was directed more and more toward politics. Working for the OUCA became all-consuming. Since she did every job that no one else wanted to do, her male colleagues began to depend on her. Eventually, she was asked to give speeches in public. This brought her to the attention of her political friends and led to her election as president of OUCA—the second woman ever to hold that position.

The Conservative Club, with 1,750 members, was the largest at Oxford. "She became president," said the male secretary to OUCA, "because of her obvious abilities: a good organizer, extremely capable, intelligent and sociable." The fact that she was a woman didn't seem to make any difference, according to the same gentleman. And apparently, the OUCA board, composed of all males, did not object to her suggestions or her style of management.

The student presidency of OUCA was to be the start of her future career. Margaret met all the visiting politicians who came to Oxford to deliver speeches in the town or informal talks to the students. She arranged dinners and parties for them, and found herself the center of political attention. In 1945, she worked to elect Conservative Quinton Hogg to represent Oxford in Parliament, but he was opposed by a Labourite who eventually won.

"One Christmas when we were home from Oxford," Margaret said, "we were at a party. After it was all over, we went into the kitchen to talk things over when a friend said to me, 'What you'd really like to do is be an MP, wouldn't you?' I replied, 'Yes, but I don't know whether it's possible. Members of Parliament don't earn very much [about $20 a week then].' "

Mr. Roberts had taught Margaret to respect the British parliamentary system, which governs and represents the British Isles: England, Scotland, Ireland, and Wales. Like most Britons, she was proud of the monarchy—a ruling king or queen, with mainly ceremonial duties—and the two houses of Parliament: the House of Lords, the upper house; and the House of Commons, the lower house. The elected members of the House of Commons propose and pass most of the legislation, while the House of Lords, whose seats are inherited, or appointed, can hold back the passage of laws up to a year before sending them to the queen for signing.

At the time of the general election in 1945, George Worth, the Conservative candidate from Grantham, asked Margaret if she would work on his campaign over the summer, and she did. He wanted her to warm up his audiences before he appeared to speak. She succeeded in raising the enthusiasm of the crowds to a high pitch of emotion just before Mr. Worth made his entrance to speak. Although the Labour party and its candidate won in Grantham, her experience was not wasted.

In 1946, as her days at Oxford drew to a close, Margaret received her bachelor of science

Margaret (top row, center), *appears with her class at Somerville College shortly before graduation.*

degree and her master of arts. Because she was los-ing interest in chemistry, her marks were not as high as she had hoped, but good nevertheless. As soon as she graduated from Oxford, she said to her good friend Margaret Goodrich. "You know, I oughtn't to have read chemistry. I should have read law. That's what I need for politics. I shall just have to go and read law now."

However, she had to find a job to support her-self before she could study law. Margaret was hired by British Xylonite Plastics, which was located sixty-nine miles northeast of London in Manning-tree, Essex. She found a room to rent in nearby

Colchester and commuted to her new job.

For the first time in its history, the company had hired three women from Oxford. The factory produced celluloid and plastic tubing. The women were placed in the research and development area and were supposed to teach the factory workers how to use the newly developed materials.

The men had a hard time taking direction from women who were young university graduates. They resented them, particularly Margaret Roberts. The other two women had a more casual approach; they could joke with the men and get them to do whatever they wanted. Margaret Roberts had a more direct way of dealing with people. The men nicknamed her "Duchess" or "Aunty Margaret," which suggested a bossy manner for someone of her age. She appeared to treat them more like children than adults. At company parties, she always wanted to talk about politics instead of socializing.

Margaret's whole life revolved around her political activities outside the plastics factory. In Colchester she joined the local Conservative group, made up mostly of military veterans (both men and women), and the OUCA's Graduate Association, which provided a close network of old friends and good contacts.

The weekends were the most important part
of her week. She traveled anywhere to a Conservative party function, whether it be a debate, a rally,
a conference, or merely a social get-together. However, she never neglected her daytime job and was
considered reliable and conscientious.

In 1948, the Oxford Graduates Association
sent her to Llandudno in North Wales to represent
them at the annual Conservative party conference.
There, in a resort town with a festive atmosphere,
she ran into an old friend from Oxford, John
Grant. They sat down to chat together with John
Miller, chairman of the Dartford Association, and
talked about politics and who would be Dartford's candidate in the next national elections.
"We haven't got one, but we're considering getting
one," John Miller told Margaret.

Margaret's friend John Grant suddenly spoke
up. "Would you consider a woman?" Before Miller could reply, Grant encouraged Margaret to put
her name forward. She was surprised, but pleased,
and met the Dartford group at the conference. She
liked them, and they were impressed with her.
Making a formal application was the next step.
Out of twenty-six applicants—twenty-five were
male—the list was narrowed to five candidates.

The candidates were next asked to come before the selection committee to speak. When Margaret spoke, "she was so wonderful, we were amazed. They thought they should have her, but they considered it wiser for her to talk before the members as a whole. It was fireworks," recalled Mr. Raymond Woollcott, Margaret Roberts's landlord for two years. "She could speak without notes up to forty-five minutes. And if someone asked her a question she didn't know, she reached down into her case for a book and found the answer."

Dartford, a town in north Kent, had sent a Labour member to Parliament for years. The Conservatives had lost before with all types, ages, and sizes of male candidates. Why not try the attractive and talented Miss Roberts to attract Dartford's 80,000 voters?

The vote was unanimous when the committee selected Margaret to run for Parliament as the Conservative candidate. Margaret Roberts was finally on the way to fulfilling her political dreams.

Chapter/Four

Fitting Marriage into a Career

The time—February 28, 1949; the place—a hall in Erith, near Dartford; the occasion—the adoption meeting, or formal approval, of Margaret Roberts as prospective parliamentary candidate by the Dartford Conservative Association. In the hall, there was a feeling of excitement as the five hundred supporters and curious onlookers awaited the introduction of their new, young, female candidate.

Although Margaret sat calmly on the platform with the other speakers, she was very nervous. Finally, Margaret Roberts was introduced to the Conservative voters, who applauded enthusiastically. She stepped toward the table with its Tory blue banner and union jack (British flag) and began to speak.

She stood before them without a note and outlined her ideas for making Dartford a better place to live and work. They liked what she said and how she said it. Then she called for questions and answered every one to their satisfaction, impressing them with her knowledge.

Before the speeches and after the formal recognition of her candidacy, a small dinner party had been given in her honor. A young man, Denis Thatcher, had been invited to attend. At the dinner and after her successful speech, Margaret was the center of attention. Suddenly she realized how late it was and that if she were to be at work early the next morning, she must leave to catch the train back to Colchester. Someone suggested to Mr. Thatcher that he take her to the Liverpool Street Station on his way back to London, which he did. That night, sliding into the seat of his Jaguar automobile, Margaret began a relationship with the tall, handsome man who was ten years older than herself, and who would eventually become her husband.

Romance, however, had to take second place to her political ambitions. She had to find a place to live in Dartford to show her voters she cared, and another job nearer the city. Margaret wanted to spend every spare evening and weekend working for her political cause.

Within a month, she found a room in a boarding house, a new job at J. Lyons and Company in Hammersmith, London, and was volunteering nights to organize political fund-raisers and rallies. Her hard work made her well liked by her co-workers.

Lucy and Raymond Woollcott, a couple in the Conservative party in Dartford, befriended her. When meetings lasted until very late at night, Mr. Woollcott would drive her home to the little room on Darenth Road where she was living, far away from the bus and train stations. He thought Margaret should be living in better conditions, so he told his wife, and they invited Margaret to live in their three-bedroom house. She accepted. "Some young men in the Conservative party helped her move in trucks and cars," said Mr. Woollcott.

For nearly two years Margaret lived with the Woollcotts, and her routine was the same: catch a bus at 6:45 A.M., change to the train going to Charing Cross Station in London, and board another bus to Hammersmith and J. Lyons. At the end of the day, she took the same means of transportation home, except she walked from the train station. Mrs. Woollcott would have dinner waiting for her before she rushed off to a political meeting.

For almost two years, Margaret lived in the Dartford home of Raymond and Lucy Woollcott.

"If ever she was going to be late or wouldn't be coming home for dinner, she would telephone ahead of time. Margaret was always very thoughtful. She wouldn't let my wife get up in the morning to prepare her breakfast," Mr. Woollcott recalled. "Because she read very late and had so many books, I turned the third bedroom into a study for her. She was like a daughter to us—always loving and affectionate."

Sometimes, Mr. and Mrs. Roberts and Muriel came down from Grantham to see her so that Alfred Roberts could speak on her behalf at political meetings.

Margaret campaigned hard against Norman Dodds, the Labour candidate. According to Margaret Phillimore, Dodds "was a charming man, who had been in the RAF [Royal Air Force] and was a journalist....They were friendly opponents." Since Dartford had long favored the Labour party, Margaret Roberts knew what a struggle she had ahead of her. Still, she had never been one to be frightened of a challenge.

She campaigned hard against Dodds on the issues, but when the polls closed in February 1950 and the votes were counted, Margaret had lost the election. She tried bravely to conceal her feelings of disappointment. There was no need to be ashamed, though; the Conservatives had made a better showing in Dartford than they ever had. Dodds received 38,128 votes to Margaret's 24,409. The British Labour party won throughout Great Britain that year, and Clement Atlee was to be the next prime minister.

The experience of defeat did not stop or discourage Margaret. She was determined to try a second time for the Dartford seat. She decided she would work harder to win, even if it took another three or four years of knocking on doors, visiting factories, and shaking thousands of hands. People in Dartford still vividly remember her personal visits to greet and talk with them.

She did all this while continuing to work full-time at J. Lyons as a research chemist, making sure food processing was safe and clean. Although she never neglected her duties, her energies were focused on politics. Her job was the only way to support herself and her political interests.

Throughout her time in Dartford, the romantic attachment with Denis Thatcher was growing. "When Denis began coming to the house to pick up Margaret, we knew this was something more than a political attachment," said Mr. Woollcott.

Denis Thatcher was from a fairly wealthy family of a respectable social class. He was considered a desirable young man for marriage, although he had been married briefly before the war and was divorced as soon as he returned. He had been a major in the Royal Artillery in France and Italy during World War II.

Denis's grandfather had been a farmer in Kent who had discovered two different chemical combinations: one for a sheep-dip and the other for a weed killer. Over the years, the successful family business expanded into paint and wallpaper. When Margaret and Denis met, he worked at the headquarters of Atlas Preservatives, in Erith near Dartford. He lived in London and commuted every day.

After a time, Margaret and Denis became very serious about marriage and were about to announce their plans when politics interfered. A general election was called by Prime Minister Clement Atlee in Ocober 1951.

The young couple's marriage plans had to be put aside as Margaret once again decided to run for Parliament. The Dartford Conservative Association was afraid her voters would think she was not a serious candidate if she had a husband and family.

She increased her political efforts in Dartford and tried to impress the voters with her intelligence and commitment. Because she was a woman, the press gave her a greater share of coverage, and she tried to take full advantage of the publicity.

Sadly, she lost a second time. As Margaret stood before the Conservative voters of Dartford, trying to hide her disappointment, Denis jumped onto the platform and announced publicly that he and Margaret were engaged to be married. Still trying to recover from Margaret's political defeat, the Dartford audience was surprised, but responded cheerfully to the couple's happy news.

Outsiders gossiped that Margaret and Denis seemed to have very little in common, to which Margaret replied, "He was in the paint and chemical business. I was a chemist. He was on the financial side, I was interested in economics. We were both interested in politics. We have a lot in common."

Margaret proudly took Denis to Grantham to meet her parents, who were now living in a semi-detached house with a garden, and to meet a few selected friends. He, in turn, introduced Margaret to his mother and sister. According to reports, the parents on both sides were uncertain about the match. Some said Margaret's parents felt that by marrying a divorced man, she was sacrificing her career, while others said Denis's mother may have felt her son was marrying beneath his social class.

Denis and Margaret Thatcher on their wedding day.

None of these concerns stopped the couple from doing what they wanted. They were married in Wesley's Chapel on London's City Road on December 13, 1951. The reception, held in a political friend's house on that foggy night, was for a small group of intimate friends.

Even Margaret's wedding dress caused criticism by the press in later years. For her, the traditional white dress for a bride was not suitable on a cold December day. She chose a velvet dress in sapphire blue (the Conservative color) that was copied from a gown worn by the Duchess of Devonshire in a painting by Sir Joshua Reynolds. Instead of wearing a wedding veil, she wore a matching blue hat with a large feather swept dramatically to one side and a velvet muff for her hands.

Except for some business that Denis had to attend to along the way, the newlyweds spent a carefree honeymoon in Portugal, Madeira, and Paris before returning to Denis's sixth floor apartment on Flood Street in London's Chelsea area. He continued to commute to Erith, but encouraged his new wife to study law.

For the time being, Margaret Thatcher put aside her desire for a parliamentary seat, and concentrated on becoming a lawyer. She had the choice of working to become a solicitor or a barrister. A solicitor would take cases and give advice, while a barrister would present cases in court. Margaret had never been a passive person. Giving advice was not enough to challenge her—she wanted the thrill of argument and debate that she had enjoyed in school and at Oxford University. For her there was only one choice—to become a barrister.

Every day Thatcher went to The Temple, or Courts of Law, at the entrance of Fleet Street, where the solicitors and barristers are clustered together in a compound of four buildings. There she was tutored at Lincoln's Inn in tax law and began her two-year study to become a barrister.

While studying law, Margaret began to express her opinions about the obstacles women faced in politics and other fields. In 1952, she wrote an article protesting this, saying, "Should a woman arise equal to the task, I say let her have an equal chance with the men for leading cabinet posts. Why not a woman chancellor or foreign secretary?"

Nothing swayed Margaret from her drive to win, though—not even her pregnancy in 1953. When she was five months pregnant, she took the first of two law exams and passed.

At the birth of her twins, Mark and Carol, Thatcher said she thought to herself in the hospital, "If I don't pursue the law, I'll let it all go. I ought to do both—law and the family. From my hospital bed, I wrote off for the papers to take the final exam. I thought pride would make me go back."

When the twins were only four months old, she went for her final examination to the bar and passed. The term *bar* comes from the ancient law courts that had a railing enclosing the lawyers when the prisoners were brought to the courtroom. The railing was like a brass or wooden bar.

Margaret Thatcher with the twins, Carol and Mark, in 1954.

From that *bar* probably came *barrister*—a lawyer standing at the bar in court, defending clients.

Denis Thatcher was completely supportive of his wife and proud of her accomplishments, both as a mother and as a barrister. Fortunately, the Thatchers had the financial means to hire a nanny to care for the twins while Margaret furthered her career. "It was Denis's money that helped me on my way," Thatcher later admitted.

Thatcher worked for six months in a tax firm, but was then told her services were no longer needed. Some say this was due to the fact that she was a woman and had entered a field dominated by men. Also, men in the 1950s did not like the idea of a mother leaving her home and children to go out to work.

This setback did not stop Margaret. She looked for another place to practice law. C.A.J. Bonner's tax firm was willing to try her out, and she stayed there until 1961. She also joined the Society of Conservative Lawyers and served on the Executive Committee from 1955 to 1957 as its first woman.

Meanwhile, the twins were growing, and the family needed more space. The Thatchers rented the apartment across the hall and cut through the wall to make one large apartment. Denis and Margaret had their own private wing, while the nanny and the twins had theirs. Margaret left the office every day at 5:30 to spend time with the children at dinner and before bedtime.

As a barrister, wife, and mother, Margaret Thatcher was still not satisfied. Her one cherished desire had not yet been fulfilled—to become a member of Parliament.

She had the opportunity to fulfill that desire when Sir John Crowther decided to retire, making his Conservative seat available to eager politicians in the wealthy Finchley district outside London. Margaret Thatcher was one of two hundred politicians who wanted to win the vacant seat. Hoping to make her long-held dream a reality, she applied. After the list had been narrowed to three candidates, Thatcher was selected and formally adopted by the Finchley constituents.

As a candidate for Finchley, Margaret had to convince the voters that she was prepared to be a member of Parliament. In one of her most important speeches of the race, given at Christ's Church College, she spoke before a large group of Finchley voters. The Labour and Liberal candidates spoke first. According to the owner of a bookstore in Finchley, when Margaret spoke, "Her address was received by tumultuous [loud] applause. She made more sense than anybody else."

Fortunately, before this new development, Margaret and Denis had decided to move outside of London to give the family more space. They found a house with four bedrooms in Farnborough, Kent, which was exactly within the forty-mile radius required by the Finchley constituency.

Working as a barrister in London, Margaret had to devote nights and weekends to political events. Her pattern was the same as it had been in Dartford, but this time she had a family to consider, too. Sometimes, Margaret took six-year-old Carol with her on a political outing. One day, Carol reportedly said to her mother before a speech, "You won't make too long a speech, will you, Mummy?"

On October 8, 1959, a few days before her thirty-fourth birthday, Margaret Thatcher was elected as a Conservative member of Parliament by a comfortable margin of three thousand votes. No one could have been prouder of Margaret than Alfred Roberts. He had trained her well. Because of his strong interest in politics, her dream was his dream, too. The young woman from Grantham had made it—she was an MP at last.

Chapter / Five

Conquering Parliament

The world's most famous clock tower soars 320 feet above the Thames River into London's silvery sky. The first morning of her MP duties, Margaret Thatcher listened to Big Ben's clanging tones as she closed her car door. Outside the houses of Parliament, she hesitated a moment to look up at the neo-Gothic building, its limestone face weathered in burnt brown and sooty black.

Stepping across the arched threshold into the octagonal (eight-sided) central lobby, she heard her footsteps echo in the vaulted mosaic ceiling above. Margaret paused to look at each of the four white statues and the four mosaic wall paintings of the patron saints of England, Scotland, Ireland, and Wales.

As Thatcher walked down the corridor on her way to the House of Commons, she felt a quiet sense of pride in her country's respect for government and law, which had lasted through the centuries. The halls and chambers inspired a certain reverence in Margaret, similar to what she felt inside a church.

Before reaching the offices for Conservative members, she looked quickly into the rectangular House of Commons, where the six hundred members gathered for formal sessions. She observed the speaker's chair and the clerk's desk at the end of the room between the two sets of parallel benches, rising like church pews in oak and jade-green leather. The government benches were to the right of the speaker's chair, and those of the opposition to the left. Her eyes lifted to the four galleries upstairs where the public, special visitors, and the press sat.

Between the two opposing sides was a large, beautifully carved mace (a wooden staff, decorated in gold), mounted at the end of the big oak table. The mace was used in the Middle Ages to keep the members from fighting each other, as were the thick red lines drawn on the carpets in front of the benches. These were reminders not to leap across the aisle to attack an opposition member during an

The Parliamentary clock tower. When the clock face is lit, it means the House of Commons is in session.

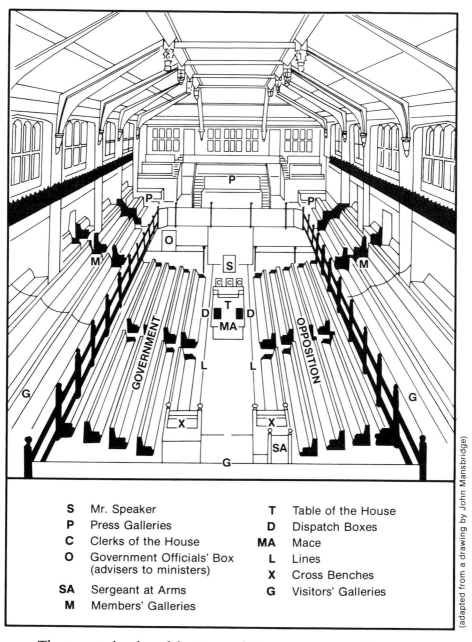

S	Mr. Speaker	**T**	Table of the House
P	Press Galleries	**D**	Dispatch Boxes
C	Clerks of the House	**MA**	Mace
O	Government Officials' Box (advisers to ministers)	**L**	Lines
		X	Cross Benches
SA	Sergeant at Arms	**G**	Visitors' Galleries
M	Members' Galleries		

(adapted from a drawing by John Mansbridge)

The present chamber of the House of Commons was opened in 1950, replacing the one that was destroyed during the London Blitz in 1941.

angry debate, and to hold tempers in check.

Thatcher also noted the two rectangular brass boxes opposite each other on either side of the oak table. These were the despatch boxes where opposing debaters would face each other. Here, the front benchers (senior members) would disrespectfully prop their feet on the table.

Margaret looked to where she would sit on the long back bench of darker green leather. For a moment, she found it hard to believe she was actually a member of Parliament for Finchley.

She hurried to find her place to work. For newly elected "back benchers," the office space was cramped and not very grand. In fact, secretaries and desks had to be shared. Margaret wasted no time in finding herself a suitable secretary, Paddi Victor Smith. Ms. Smith agreed to become her part-time secretary and fully expected to have to show Thatcher what to do. That first impression was wrong. Margaret took charge right away, and Ms. Smith rarely had any free time after that.

Traditionally, "back benchers" put their names in a hat for a drawing to select someone to introduce a private member's bill. This way, no favorites are chosen to speak. By chance and to her astonishment, Thatcher's name was drawn soon after she started her term.

A topic had to be chosen quickly, and the research gathered hastily. Margaret picked the Public Bodies Bill, proposing that the press be allowed to attend local council meetings, from which they had always been barred.

The time set for giving her first speech in the House of Commons couldn't have been worse—a Friday afternoon. Members usually left early for a weekend in the country, for parties, or for relaxing after a morning session on Friday. But that Friday afternoon, many of them stayed to hear the new member from Finchley deliver her opening speech.

When Margaret Thatcher rose to speak, a hush fell over the House of Commons. Because a female MP was so unusual in the 1960s, all eyes were on the thirty-four-year-old woman. She carefully covered up her nervousness, and then spoke for almost an hour without a note, trying to persuade the MPs to open council meetings to reporters. After her final words, applause filled the chamber. Comments from opponents were favorable: "A speech of front bench quality" and "a fluency most of us would envy."

Members of the press who had listened to Thatcher's speech from the galleries were overjoyed. Outside, they snapped dozens of photographs and hurried to get interviews. Margaret was their champion, their new celebrity. The honeymoon between the press and this new politician was underway. Margaret had no idea her choice of proposed legislation would cause such a stir.

This first exposure to fame and success had no effect on Thatcher's daily routine. She made breakfast for Denis every morning and saw that the children were dressed properly before going to school. While Denis drove his car to Erith for work, Margaret commuted to London in her little blue car and sometimes dropped the children at school.

Work began at the House of Commons early in the morning and often didn't finish until 10:00 or 10:30 P.M., although the formal meetings in the Commons did not start until 2:30 in the afternoon.

Mornings for Thatcher were spent writing letters and speeches, talking with voters from Finchley, reading periodicals, or giving interviews. Even her visits to the hairdresser were opportunities to dictate to her secretary while under the dryer.

Margaret lunched in either the canteen or the member's dining room, where she developed a reputation for eating at top speed. To prevent opposing members from eavesdropping on conversations, the dining room was divided in half: one side for Conservatives, and the other for Labourites. The green carpet in the hall was for the House of Commons area, and the red carpet for the House of Lords.

Thatcher's afternoons and evenings were devoted to the sessions in the House of Commons and to the prime minister's question time on Tuesdays and Thursdays. She was seldom home for dinner, but she called her children every evening to talk with them and say goodnight. Denis worked late at his office, too, but they were both available by telephone for the children if any emergency occurred. When Mark and Carol played with neighborhood children, they couldn't understand what other mothers did at home all day.

Margaret's philosophy about the home went like this, "Life doesn't revolve around your home. Home is a base from which you go out and do your own thing, whether it be work or some other sort of activity."

Although she wasn't at home to supervise them all the time, the education of her children was very important to Margaret Thatcher. Mark went to boarding school at eight years of age, which is standard for most British children from upper-class families. He attended Belmont, Mill Hill (where his father attended), and Harrow. At age ten, Carol was sent to boarding school at

Thatcher in 1961 as a Conservative member of Parliament for Finchley.

Queenswood. Both children had all the advantages
Margaret never had in her childhood, such as dancing and riding lessons.

"When you have children," said Thatcher,
"your attitude changes. You are living for another
human being. Someone else matters more than
yourself. You give children what you didn't have. I
tried to give my children more amusement, sport,
and theater."

During her early years as an MP, the Thatcher
family managed to take a vacation at the seaside in
summer on the Isle of Wight. Later, they started
skiing in Switzerland during the Christmas holidays. Margaret liked the slower pace for a time,
but she was never very good at being idle and
would return early to get back to work.

Her first two years as an MP were filled with
long hours of research and proposals for certain
bills. She did the research herself; memorizing her
material and writing in longhand, she had a keen
grasp of her subjects. The only real handicap she
had was her nervousness before speaking. That
never left her. Yet her habit of thorough research
and her respect for her topic, both learned at Kesteven, helped her overcome her fear.

"She had a knack for skimming over para-
graphs and getting the meat and meaning out of

what she read," said Raymond Woollcott, her friend and landlord from Dartford. "I don't know how she did it."

Her ideas and opinions were definite, and she was not afraid to express them. On the Criminal Justice Bill, she wanted to see murderers receive the death penalty (corporal punishment) in order to protect the public. Her study of tax law proved useful, especially when she wanted the surtax (an extra tax) reduced for married women who wanted to work.

"Super Mac" began to notice her after her two years as an MP; that was the nickname for the Conservative prime minister, Harold Macmillan. One day he called Thatcher into his office and asked her to be parliamentary secretary to the Ministry of Pensions and National Insurance, a position which she accepted and held from 1961 to 1964. Her surprise and joy at being recognized were saddened by the fact that her mother died of cancer in December 1960 before she knew of her daughter's appointment.

"My mother was practical," Margaret recalled. "She worked hard. She backed up Daddy in everything he did and she would say, 'Your father had a difficult day standing up for his principles.'"

Whatever assignment Margaret Thatcher was

given, she learned all she possibly could about it. Reviewing every speech and paper written about pensions and welfare from the years 1946 to 1962 gave her knowledge beyond most other members. Her speech on pensions was so well prepared and so full of statistics and facts that no one could reply convincingly.

Meanwhile, the British economy was weakening, and unemployment was rising. Despite Harold Macmillan's earlier popularity, his own cabinet joined members of the opposition to complain about his leadership. Although Margaret was unhappy with Macmillan's economic policies, she remained loyal. In July 1963, Harold Macmillan called for the resignation of most of his cabinet. This was known as the "July Massacre."

New people in the cabinet didn't help the country's problems, though. On October 18, 1963, Harold Macmillan stepped aside so that Sir Alec Douglas-Home (pronounced Hume) could become the Conservative leader and prime minister.

Yet after only a year of the new leadership, Home called a nationwide election. Usually, the prime minister calls a general election by going to the queen and asking her to dissolve Parliament. Each party is then allowed to campaign three or four weeks before the new election.

Because the Finchley voters were unhappy with the Conservative government, too, Margaret had a difficult time persuading them to return her to Parliament. Eventually, they did, but with a much smaller majority than she had had before. For Margaret, Finchley could no longer be taken for granted. She refused to change her views, however, saying "there's only one way, you've got to go out on the streets and fight them and be Conservative, and you'll win in the end."

The election was a close one, but Labour Leader Harold Wilson and his party won. Margaret and the Conservatives retreated to the opposition side of the House of Commons until 1970.

The Tories searched for a new leader to give them a stronger image. Edward Heath, who had been the minister of labor, was their choice, and Margaret, too, supported him for leader of the party.

While her political life remained unsettled, Margaret somehow managed to keep her home life stable. She and Denis lived in an apartment in Westminster Gardens near the House of Commons and rented a cottage not too far from a golf course for weekends. Two years later, Denis's family business was sold, allowing them to sell their Kent house and buy one in Lamberhurst. The new house was on three acres of land with a tennis court and a swimming pool.

Margaret's happiness about the new house was forgotten, however, when she received news that her father had become ill. She immediately went to Grantham to be with him. Eventually, Alf Roberts recovered, and he married a neighboring widow with four grown children in 1965. Knowing he would not be alone was a comfort to Margaret.

Thatcher's political knowledge continued to grow under Ted Heath's leadership of the Conservative party. She was assigned a variety of posts in the shadow cabinet. Under the British political system, the party not in power appoints a shadow minister—a minister who does not serve in the government—to correspond to the officials who actually occupy all government posts. Margaret served in social security, housing and land, treasury matters, fuel and power, and education.

In her shadow cabinet position at treasury, Thatcher joined the rest of the Conservative party in criticizing the Labour government's financial problems and debts. She told the public it was time that Britain "stood on its own two feet."

Partly due to this criticism, Ted Heath and his Conservative party defeated Harold Wilson in the 1970 general election and were back in power.

This time Margaret won her Finchley seat with an overwhelming majority. "She always got things done," explained one voter.

Before the day of the election, however, Alf Roberts died in Grantham. Margaret experienced enormous grief; the emptiness she felt after her father's death was almost unbearable. Unfortunately, her father did not live long enough to know about the successful election or her appointment by Ted Heath as secretary of state for education and science, and as privy counsellor (private adviser) to the prime minister. He would have been pleased, though not surprised, by her achievements.

"He brought me up to believe all the things I do believe and they're the values on which I fought the election. I owe almost everything to my father," she said in her time of sorrow.

Thatcher coped with her grief inwardly and went back to work. Her new office at the Department of Education and Science was comfortable and spacious. A government car was provided for her, but her comfort didn't slow her desire to learn everything there was to know about the flaws in Britain's educational system. She insisted that children not be allowed to drop out of school before the age of sixteen. This decision was the first of many which would anger certain sections of the public and the opposition.

If Thatcher's educational policies created some enemies outside her party, her ambition and aggressiveness didn't make many friends in her own cabinet, either. In fact, her speech before five thousand women made her unpopular with her own party leader, Ted Heath. She told the women of the National Union of Townwomen's Guilds in Albert Hall, "If you want something said, ask a man. If you want something done, ask a woman." The women in the audience loved it and applauded wildly. The phrase made headlines and was widely repeated on television and radio in Great Britain. It also made her party members angry.

Her next step, as minister of education in 1970, created such a scandal that her political career was nearly destroyed. That year, the Tories decided to cut the education budget. Margaret fought hard against it, but in the end she had to take £8 million from her budget. To reduce it that much, she cut free milk from schools for children ages seven to eleven.

The country went into an uproar. The press called her a "milk snatcher," and cartoonists made endless fun of her in their drawings. The Labourites in the House of Commons were delighted.

Here was an opportunity to criticize Thatcher. Through all the controversy, Denis tried to shield his wife as best he could, both physically and mentally. However, during a speech she was giving in a small town, someone threw a stone that hit her in the chest. Hiding the pain, she kept speaking. Parents and students in the crowd were angry and rude. Even students at the University of London unfairly took out their anger on Margaret's daughter, Carol.

Margaret Thatcher had no idea the "milk scandal" would cause such a reaction. "I took the view that most parents are able to pay for milk for their children, and that the job of the government was to provide such things in education which they couldn't pay for like new primary schools," Thatcher explained. "The previous Labour government had stopped free milk in secondary school and though some on their own side objected, there was no great storm over that. The important thing was to protect education, and that's what we did. Indeed, we expanded it."

She did not back down or give up on her legislation, but the "honeymoon" with the press was over. At one point, Denis asked why she didn't "chuck it all in." She sighed and said, "I can't, I still have too much to do."

Great Britain was in trouble, and so was Ted Heath. Prices were going up, workers were striking for more money, and Heath's decision to national- ize some industries (to make them government- owned and run) upset his own party members. Nationalization was against Conservative party philosophy. By February 1974, Heath was forced to call an election. The Labour party under Harold Wilson once again was returned to power.

Margaret managed to be re-elected in Finchley, but since the party now was the opposition, she had to give up her large office and go back to a small room. In spite of the milk scandal, Heath appointed Thatcher to the shadow cabinet as a front-bencher to speak about the environment and treasury matters; she was valuable to the party.

At this time the Conservative party was un- dergoing a crisis of leadership. The members did not like Ted Heath's style and felt he was a weak leader. Someone jokingly mentioned Marga- ret Thatcher's name. She laughed and said, "It will be years before a woman either leads the party or becomes prime minister. I don't see it happening in my lifetime."

However, a few months later, after deciding that none of the other Conservative candidates was worthy of the position, she let her name be

Thatcher and her 21-year-old-son, Mark, during her campaign for Conservative party leader.

SUNDAY EXPRESS

1,500 Young Tories stand and cheer...

BATTLING MARGARET
GRABS HER CHANCE

Garages

considered. Gordon Reece, a journalist and pro-
ducer, had met Margaret Thatcher while he was
making political broadcasts for the Tories. He
thought she had all the right qualities to be leader.
To help her appeal to the people of Great Britain,
he suggested that she try to improve her relationship with the press.

Another supporter, Airey Neave, an old friend,
agreed to be her campaign manager. Neave said
Margaret was "The first new idealist politician for
a long time....a philosopher as well as a politician." With the support and encouragement of
Reece, Neave, and her family, Margaret Thatcher
entered the race for leader of the Conservative
party.

Chapter/Six

"Now I Am Leader"

Margaret Thatcher had been waiting in Airey Neave's office for the final election results that February night in 1975. She would never forget his serious face and his words as he strolled into his office and calmly said, "It's all right. You're leader of the opposition."

The agony was over. She sighed with relief and for a few moments shared her joy with friends and campaign workers before taking care of all the details facing her as the new leader. Her thoughts turned to a press conference that she must hold almost immediately.

After making a few notes, she was ready to face the media. The television cameras focused on her as she approached them. Flashbulbs snapped

Thatcher greets a crowd of reporters after being elected Tory leader.

and cameras clicked. The volume was turned high on the microphones, and reporters held their notebooks and pens ready to quote her words.

"To me it is a dream that the next name in the list after Harold Macmillan, Sir Alec Douglas-Home, and Edward Heath is Margaret Thatcher," she told the reporters and the viewers. "Each has brought his own style of leadership and stamp of greatness to his task, and I shall take on the work with humility and dedication. There is much to do, and I hope you will allow me the time to do it thoughtfully and well."

At midnight when she reached her apartment

at Flood Street, the press and public were camped outside on the steps and in the street, waiting for the new leader's appearance.

Margaret Thatcher was no longer a private citizen. The press would shadow her every move, looking for fresh story lines and exclusive photos. As reporters began digging up all the personal details about the Tory leader, they stumbled on a fact that had not surfaced before—Denis Thatcher's divorce in 1946 after returning from the war. The Thatcher twins had no idea of their father's previous marriage until they read it in the newspapers. With typical British reserve, neither parent had ever referred to that part of their past. They considered it a whirlwind war marriage and not that important.

Next, Thatcher called upon Ted Heath at his home as a matter of courtesy to offer him any position in the shadow cabinet he wanted. Feeling bitter and rejected from his loss, he refused to take any part in the Thatcher opposition. His defeat by a woman had wounded his pride.

Putting together a shadow cabinet and placing the right people in key positions was Margaret's next job. There were twenty-two places to fill. Naturally, she wanted her own supporters around her, but Mr. Heath had some capable people whom she needed. With skill and diplomacy, she fired seven and kept others in positions where she could watch them and not worry about their being too close to her inner circle.

Because of the pressures on her time, she needed a speech writer. Gordon Reece—now her public relations adviser—suggested she use Ronald Millar, an actor and playwright who had worked on Ted Heath's speeches for years. Understandably, Margaret did not want to hire someone whose loyalties had been to Heath. She wanted someone committed to her, but Gordon Reece insisted that they meet anyway. Reluctantly, she agreed.

The chemistry between Thatcher and Millar seemed to work. After meeting him, she asked him to prepare a five-minute political broadcast for her. He wrote it backstage and returned to read it while she listened politely. The speech ended with a quotation from Abraham Lincoln.

> You cannot bring about prosperity by discouraging thrift.
>
> You cannot strengthen the weak by weakening the strong.
>
> You cannot help strong men by tearing down big men.
>
> You cannot further the brotherhood of man by encouraging class hatred.

You cannot help the poor by destroying the rich.

You cannot establish sound security on borrowed money.

You cannot keep out of trouble by spending more than you earn.

You cannot build character and courage by taking away man's initiative and independence.

You cannot help men permanently by doing for them what they could and should do for themselves.

Thatcher pulled a worn piece of paper folded inside her wallet and handed it to Ronald Millar. He opened it. That exact quotation from Lincoln, which she always carried with her, was written on it. Without any more questions, Mr. Millar was put on the staff as a speech writer, although he was not the only one she would use. She wanted at least four or five different speeches written before she chose the one she liked best. These had to be printed and distributed to the press and politicians, which meant she could not speak without notes as she had done in the past.

The rooms for the leader of the opposition were grander than any she had worked in during the last fifteen years. They were spacious and

impressive, except for the view from the large window over the parking lot. Margaret, who had always enjoyed redecorating, furnished her offices in a more feminine, but businesslike atmosphere.

Another personnel matter was her driver, who came with the job as leader of the Conservative party. George Newell had driven Ted Heath for years, and Margaret wasn't sure whether she should keep him or find another. She decided to let him stay on as her driver, and he became devoted to her. Often he would be required to work late at night or on weekends, keeping him away from his family. This greatly troubled Margaret, and she frequently gave him flowers to take home to his wife. She was also fond of the detectives who were now assigned to guard her every move.

Knowing the importance of her physical appearance for television and newspaper interviews, Gordon Reece began working on her wardrobe, her hairstyle, her makeup, her weight, and lowering the pitch of her voice.

With all this added responsibility, keeping her family unified was important to her. Her secretary and Denis's secretary tried hard to coordinate the couple's schedules as best they could.

When Denis decided to retire at the age of sixty, Margaret said, "I don't know what I'm going

With a bowl of flowers to brighten her new office, Thatcher leaves her home in Flood Street.

to do when Denis retires. He can't retire. He must find something to do." Despite her doubts, his appointment to several business boards and his golf playing kept him well occupied. His freer schedule also made it possible for him to accompany Margaret on political trips.

Travel would become a vital part of Thatcher's position as leader as she tried to overcome the weak point in her political experience—foreign affairs. Though her knowledge of other countries was lacking, she was determined to correct this and learn as much as she could by reading and traveling. After twelve trips around her own country when the House of Commons was out of session, she made three trips overseas.

One of these trips was to the United States in September 1975. There she made numerous appearances in New York City, where she spoke to foreign policy groups, businessmen and women, the United Nations ambassadors, and attended many parties given in her honor.

"An ounce of contact is worth a ton of reading," said Thatcher. "I think the head of a major party should know other world leaders personally because you always learn in those face-to-face discussions."

With her travels abroad and her recognition in

the United States by President Gerald Ford and
Secretary of State Henry Kissinger, she felt more
secure in foreign affairs. "I feel I have been accepted as a leader in the international sphere—
the field in which they said I would never be
accepted."

Television interviews were part of the daily
schedule for distinguished foreign visitors to America. Margaret Thatcher was no exception. Barbara
Walters, a skillful interviewer, invited her to appear on the *Today* show. Walter's first impression
of Thatcher was a surprise. "She was prettier than
I expected, softer, younger. She was perfectly love-
ly and charming."

Walters warned Thatcher that she would have
to ask her some questions about achieving high office as a woman. The two women, both successful
in their own right, compared notes on this subject,
which they both disliked discussing. Thatcher answered her by saying, "Isn't it too bad that there
aren't more women around who feel as we do?"

Thatcher's daughter, Carol, was one of these
women. Back in England, she passed her law exams at the University of London and decided to go
to Chichester to qualify as a solicitor. Even though
Carol was an adult, her mother still worried about
where she lived, what she ate, if she were warm

enough, and if she had enough money.

To Margaret's great disappointment, her son, Mark, turned down a place at Oxford University to join an Australian accounting firm. He did not like to study and had difficulty passing exams. "University—undreamed of for my father; my dream; my son's refusal. All in three generations," she said with a note of regret. Mark's interest was in car racing, a fact which always worried his mother.

As for her husband, reporters tried again and again to interview Denis Thatcher. He made it a policy, though, not to give interviews. "They say I am the most shadowy husband of all time. I intend to stay that way and leave the limelight to my wife." He seemed quite happy to stay in the background, playing golf or watching rugby, soccer, or cricket.

In October, the Conservative party conference was held at the seaside in the city of Blackpool. It would be Margaret Thatcher's first as its new leader and was crucial to her future acceptance. Because her election had caused some bad feelings within the party, she was uneasy about the week of meetings to come. She had to gain the support of all the party members.

The day after she arrived, Ted Heath made

an unexpected appearance at the conference. He talked openly to friends and reporters, telling them that Margaret Thatcher would ruin the Conservative party. Heath's arrival and his comments were working against her effort to inspire and lead her party.

The major event of the conference would be her speech on Friday morning. She quickly asked Ronald Millar to come down from London to help her with a new speech. In a state of worry and nerves, Thatcher and Millar worked all Thursday night, preparing for the challenge she would soon have to face.

Chapter/Seven

"Britain Needs an Iron Lady"

Friday morning came all too soon. Before Margaret left the hotel room, Denis squeezed her hand. He may have been more nervous than she was.

Waiting on the platform to speak, Thatcher appeared calm, but inwardly she was dealing with nervousness and fear of the audience's response. Her future as a strong leader was at stake.

After Thatcher was introduced, she stepped forward with a feather duster that a woman had handed her from the audience and humorously dusted the lectern. Then quickly, she tickled her introducer's nose with the duster.

The audience laughed and cheered. That little moment of humor persuaded the delegates to support Margaret Thatcher.

Thatcher waves to the convention delegates after promising to "sweep out the corners of Number Ten Downing Street."

Part of her speech went like this: 'I know you will understand the humility I feel at following in the footsteps of great men like...Winston Churchill, a man called by destiny to raise the name of Britain to supreme heights in the history of the world...of Anthony Eden, who set us the goal of a property-owning democracy....of Harold Macmillan, whose leadership brought so many ambitions within the grasp of every citizen...of Alec Douglas-Home, who earned the affection and admiration of us all...and of Edward Heath, who successfully led the party to victory in 1970 and brilliantly led the nation into Europe in 1973."

She continued, "...they all had one thing in common: each met the challenge of his time. Now, what is the challenge of our time? I believe...to overcome the country's economic and financial problems, and to regain our confidence in Britain and ourselves."

Thatcher said that to do this, the country must abandon socialism. Socialism is an economic theory that promotes government-owned companies, industries, and utilities. Capitalism, on the other hand, promotes private and individual ownership separate from the government. Thatcher's father prospered as an individual owner because he worked hard. She wanted British people to have the same opportunity because she believed it would make the country stronger. This policy has become known as "Thatcherism."

In her travels abroad, Margaret Thatcher had criticized some aspects of life in Great Britain. She had to make clear what she had meant in her speech at the party conference. "It wasn't Britain I was criticizing, it was socialism; and I will go on... because it is bad for Britain. Britain and socialism are not the same thing, and as long as I have health and strength they never will be. Let me give you my vision: a man's right to work as he will, to spend what he earns, to have property, to have the state as a servant and not as a master; these are the British inheritance.''

To her relief, the audience reaction was positive. She put aside her fears and could say confidently, ''Now I am leader.''

But back in the House of Commons, Prime Minister Harold Wilson ignored most of Thatcher's questions and treated her more like a child than as an equal. He referred to her knowledge of foreign affairs in a joking manner, which irritated and frustrated Thatcher. In order to make Wilson take notice, she made a tough speech in the Commons against the Soviet Union.

''The Russians are bent on world dominance, and they are rapidly acquiring the means to become the most powerful imperial nation the world has seen. They put guns before butter, while we put just about everything before guns,'' she said.

This speech made its way back to the Kremlin (government offices) in the Soviet Union. One of the Russian news agencies, TASS, gave Margaret Thatcher a nickname that was to stick to her forever. They called her the Iron Lady and the Cold War Warrior, and she became known to the world as the Iron Lady. Cartoonists and newspaper columnists began referring to Thatcher by this new name. She was far from angry.

"That's the greatest compliment they could ever have paid me. They were right: Britain needs an iron lady," Thatcher commented.

While Margaret Thatcher was experiencing success, Prime Minister Harold Wilson was not. In 1976 he presented his resignation to the queen. There was no apparent reason, since he was not in any personal difficulty or ill health. Searching for a new leader, the Labour party chose James Callaghan, who was then foreign secretary, and elected him to become the next prime minister.

Callaghan, too, regarded Thatcher as someone not to be taken seriously. Time after time in the Commons, he would answer her question by saying, "Now, now, little lady." This phrase made her furious.

Gordon Reece came to her rescue again by hiring a television advertising agency that would make Margaret Thatcher more appealing to the British public. Reece taught her to talk closer to the microphone to create a more friendly, informal feeling. As her voice lowered, it took on a husky, appealing quality. He also persuaded her to grant interviews to help the public accept her as a woman, a mother, and a politician.

To strengthen her knowledge and experience of foreign affairs, she traveled abroad to meet

*Denis (far left) and Mark (far right) say good-bye to Carol (back)
and Margaret as they leave on a trip to the Far East.*

America's newly elected president, Jimmy Carter. She also went to China, Japan, and Hong Kong.

Meanwhile, the pressure of being Margaret Thatcher's daughter and the publicity given to her private life had become too much for Carol Thatcher. To escape, she went to Australia, intending to stay for six months. Instead, she lived there for five years as a journalist for the *Sydney Morning Herald*. Mark, too, had begun to dislike the newspaper coverage of his personal and business life. Several years later, he would move to America to live and work. Denis managed to stay out of the limelight, but he did defend his wife.

While Margaret was trying to expand her knowledge of foreign affairs, problems were mounting in England. The growing number of immigrants moving into the country was causing overcrowding in low-income housing and racial riots in many areas of the country. During the 1970s, Pakistanis, Africans, and whites fought in the streets of London and other cities.

Thatcher's solution to these racial problems was simple—stop immigration. She recognized that without some kind of limit on the number of people coming to live in Great Britain, overcrowding and racial conflict would become more and more common.

The outrage that followed her suggestion was intense. The Labour party called her inhuman and a racist; the Church of England called her unchristian; and members of her own party joined the attack.

Her response to those who opposed her was, "I'm not ruthless. Some things have to be done, and I know when they are done one will be accused of all sorts of things." She refused to change her position.

Friday, October 13, 1978, was Margaret Thatcher's birthday. As she turned fifty-three years old, she once again faced her party in Brighton for its annual conference. Thatcher and Millar worked hard on her traditional Friday speech, targeting the Labour party, or "looney left," as she called them. "When you hold back the successful, you penalize those who need help," she told her fellow Conservatives.

When Thatcher finished her speech, a cake was wheeled on stage and a Paddington bear placed in her arms. She was both pleased and surprised that they had remembered her birthday. Along with all the other events on that long day, she gave a party for the police officers who were assigned to protect her. Margaret Thatcher had a way of showing she cared for those on her staff.

A secretary said of her, "One of us would be there until the House rose or until midnight, whichever was the earliest, and I would drive her home, so tired I could barely speak after a long day, and I'd have another four days like it ahead, but we always knew that she had to go home and start on her work files. However hard any of her staff worked, she worked harder."

While Thatcher enjoyed personal popularity within her own party, Great Britain itself was in trouble again. A bitterly cold winter was made worse by industrial strikes by workers who demanded more money. Trucks wouldn't deliver oil, which meant gas pumps had no gas, trains stopped running, unheated schools closed, and garbage wasn't collected.

The British people were angry.

On March 30, 1979, Thatcher acted decisively in the House of Commons. She proposed a vote of no confidence in the government's Labour party and said, "The government has failed the nation. It has lost credibility and it's time for it to go." For seven hours, the House of Commons debated Labour's bad management of the country. When put to the vote, the Liberals added their thirteen votes to the Conservatives, and Labour lost by one vote: 311 to 310. After the debate, Prime Minister James

Callaghan asked the queen to dissolve Parliament.

When the new election date of May 3, 1979, was announced, Thatcher and her party were in high spirits. Thatcher reportedly said to Denis, "Exciting. A night like this comes once in a lifetime."

In the midst of their excitement, they were sobered by an accident that wounded and eventually killed Thatcher's close friend, Airey Neave. Thatcher had appointed him shadow secretary to Northern Ireland after she had been elected to lead the party. A group of terrorists who were opposed to Neave's views placed a bomb in his car to protest the government's policy for Northern Ireland. Margaret Thatcher could hardly believe the news. She had great respect for Airey, as did her family, and immediately wrote a public tribute to him. "The assassination of Airey Neave has left his friends and colleagues as stunned and grief-stricken as his family. He was one of freedom's warriors. Courageous, staunch, true, he lived for his beliefs and now he has died for them....Now there is a gap in our lives which cannot be filled."

After hearing the news, Carol Thatcher telephoned from Australia and said, "Oh, Mum, I'm so sorry." The mother and daughter shared their sadness with each other, and before Carol hung up, Margaret said, "We must win now. We'll win for Airey." Not long after that call, Carol returned home to help her mother during the four weeks allowed for campaigning before an election. Eventually, Carol would return to Great Britain to work as a journalist on the *Daily Express.*

Gordon Reece started his publicity campaign. He arranged interviews for Thatcher and made sure her picture was taken shopping and doing everyday things as well as on the campaign trail. On Saturdays, Denis, Carol, and Margaret went to Finchley, shaking hands and gathering support for the Conservative party. Margaret appeared tireless. "Unless we change our ways and our direction, our greatness as a nation will soon be a footnote in the history books, a distant memory of an offshore island, lost in the mists of time like Camelot, remembered kindly for its noble past," she said in a passionate campaign speech.

The press kept predicting that Labour would win. Someone suggested that Margaret Thatcher and Ted Heath should pose together in public to show unity in the Conservative party. Thatcher totally rejected the idea. Denis observed, "I've never seen her so upset, never, ever."

When election day arrived, Britain was battered by rain and snow, but 76 percent of the voting public defied the weather to cast their votes.

Margaret and Denis greet Finchley supporters after Margaret's election as the prime minister.

A nervous Margaret Thatcher waited with family and colleagues all night and part of the next day for the official count. Finally, the news came: Thatcher and her party won the very close election by 7,900 votes. Callaghan's justification for the Labour loss was, "People voted against last winter, rather than for the Conservatives."

Thatcher took very little time to congratulate herself and enjoy her achievement. She and Ronald Millar met at four in the morning to plan what she would say when she reached her new prime minister's residence, Ten Downing Street. Millar came up with a saying from St. Francis of Assissi: "Where there is discord may we bring harmony, where there is error may we bring truth, where there is doubt may we bring faith, and where there is despair, may we bring hope."

Momentarily, Margaret's eyes filled with tears. They were tears of joy, but also tears of sadness that her father, Alfred Roberts, was not there to know what she had achieved.

Not only was Margaret Thatcher the first woman to serve as leader of the Conservative party she was now the first woman to become prime minister of Great Britain. This would be a historic night to remember.

Chapter/Eight

Prime Minister: Breaking the Barriers

The most important telephone call of the election had not yet come. Once Margaret Thatcher had been officially declared the new prime minister, the queen's secretary was supposed to telephone the newly elected leader and invite her to visit the queen at Buckingham Palace, official residence of the royal family.

Margaret, Denis, Carol, and Mark Thatcher were nervously waiting for that call at the Conservative party's central offices in Smith Square, not far from the houses of Parliament. Then the telephone rang. The four Thatchers froze in silence.

Before Thatcher's secretary reached for the receiver, she whispered, "That's it!" They held their breaths; no, that wasn't it. A second call came through, but again it wasn't. When the telephone rang a third time, they were relaxed and not expecting it to be the one they were waiting for. But this time, it was. Margaret Thatcher took the call alone in a separate room. In a few minutes, she returned to announce the queen's request for her visit to Buckingham Palace.

Carol and Mark left for Ten Downing Street as Margaret and Denis stepped into a black limousine that would take them past the gates of Buckingham Palace to the royal entrance. Inside, Denis was asked to stay downstairs with the queen's aides and wait for his wife.

Thatcher was shown upstairs to the queen's study where Queen Elizabeth II was waiting to perform the "kissing hands" ceremony, a centuries-old tradition. This is the official way for the queen to ask the new prime minister if he or she is ready to form a new government. The prime minister answers "yes," and the queen gives her approval. Usually, the meeting is very brief, but Margaret Thatcher and the queen spoke for forty-five minutes. The two women appeared to have a lot to talk about at that first meeting.

Next, Margaret and Denis headed for the official prime minister's residence, Ten Downing Street, where a cheering crowd and the news media were waiting for them. Standing in the doorway, Thatcher delivered her quote from St. Francis of Assisi, paid tribute to her father, and said, "To all the British people, howsoever they may have voted, may I say this: now that the election is over, may we get together and strive to serve and strengthen the country of which we are so proud to be a part. And finally, one last thing: in the words of Airey Neave, whom we had hoped to bring here with us, 'Now there is work to be done.'"

Once the new prime minister and her staff marched through the doors with their official red briefcases and despatch boxes, the celebrating was over.

Ten Downing Street is a working office as well as a residence. Every day, more than one hundred people go to work there. The government pays for the maintenance of the building and for the salaries of the civil servants, while the prime minister pays for the household help and rent, based on 10 percent of her salary.

The living quarters of the prime minister's residence, located on the top floor, needed remodeling when the Thatchers moved in. The family stayed at their Flood Street apartment for several weeks until the work was completed.

The first order of business for Prime Minister Thatcher, meanwhile, was to choose a twenty-two-member cabinet to govern the country, which she did in two days. Instead of selecting a cabinet composed of people with many different points of view, she chose one that she knew would support her. Earlier, she had told a London *Observer* reporter that the new government "must be a conviction government....As prime minister, I couldn't waste time having any internal arguments."

She chose several of Ted Heath's men to serve on the new cabinet. Although she knew they would not always agree with her, her key choices would fully support her plans and would help convince the rest of the members.

Within twelve days of the election, Parliament was back in session with all the fanfare of a royal ceremony. The queen sat on the throne in the House of Lords, sending a messenger to the House of Commons to knock on the doors and invite the two parties to come to her. Prime Minister Thatcher with her Conservatives and Opposition Leader James Callaghan with his Labourites then met in the Lord's chamber to hear the queen's speech. Written by the newly elected prime minister, the speech outlined the government's plans.

After all the official ceremonies were over,

In the House of Commons, a messenger arrives to lead the prime minister and her cabinet to meet with the queen in the House of Lords.

Thatcher's life soon settled into a daily routine, which has remained fairly constant during more than ten years in office. After only four or five hours of sleep a night, she would read the morning papers—sometimes marked by her staff with stories of special interest—at 6:30 A.M. and listen to the radio news or watch the television news. The ritual of making breakfast for Denis stayed the same. By 8:30 A.M. she would walk downstairs into the study to plan the day with a press secretary, advisers, and her own personal secretary. Then she would attend committee meetings and a two-hour cabinet meeting on Tuesday and Thursday mornings. Every Tuesday and Thursday afternoon, the House of Commons holds a question time from 3:15 to 3:30 P.M. At that time, the opposition can ask the prime minister any question it wishes, or challenge any political decisions she has made.

Thatcher's new duties included meetings with foreign leaders and heads of industries, as well as weekly meetings with the queen (usually on Tuesday nights). There were speeches, banquets, broadcasts, and endless amounts of paperwork. Thatcher double-checked everything for accuracy. "Show me the research on which this is based," she would demand impatiently.

The prime minister's main concern during her first days in office was to live up to the words in her acceptance speech the night of her victory; it was time to "get together and strive to serve and strengthen the country." Her primary goal was to strengthen the British economy. To do this, Thatcher believed three important things must be done: lower the income tax rate, which would increase the amount of money people were earning and spending on goods and services; raise the VAT (the value added tax placed on all goods and services) by 15 percent and increase taxes on gas, alcohol, and cigarettes, which would give the government more money; and sell British Airways and

British Petroleum to private companies. Thatcher thought that by selling these government-owned corporations, the government would make money. Also, she was convinced that private owners were better able to run and manage the companies, which would benefit the people of Great Britain.

Margaret Thatcher was suddenly very unpopular. The leader of the opposition, James Callaghan, criticized the new prime minister and her plans; he wasn't the only one. Labor unions across the country, as well as members of her own party, said she had made a mistake.

Thatcher called members of the Tory party who felt she had gone too far, too fast "wets," and those who agreed with her "drys." The opposition party argued that the world economy was so weak that her decisions would cause a depression in the British economy.

Thatcher explained that she had no choice—it was the only way to "cure" the country. This statement was criticized, too, because many thought she should listen to what other members of the government had to say. The following June, Thatcher made even larger cuts in the budget that were supposed to solve the growing trade deficit (England was importing more goods than it was exporting). These budget cuts caused another wave of protest.

While Thatcher was trying to cure the country's economic problems, she realized she couldn't ignore other aspects of being a world leader. To improve her reputation in other nations, Thatcher tried to learn as much as she could about them. During her first year in office, the prime minister traveled to the United Nations in New York, and to international summits around the world. On these trips, she met other leaders, found out how they handled problems in their own countries, and explained how she handled hers. Although some of the people she met said she was too outspoken, almost all admired her courage in making such big changes during her first year in office.

After that first year, the country was still in a difficult economic and social position. Unemployment rose, and millions of people had to depend on government welfare programs. Many companies were losing money and going out of business due to the large spending cuts made by Thatcher's government. Also, the first steel strike in fifty-four years caused growing conflict in the nation. Violence broke out in the streets.

The situation in England was so bad that Harold Macmillan and Ted Heath, former prime ministers, spoke out publicly against Thatcher. They said her programs were too severe and that the changes in policy should be made more slowly to give people time to adjust.

There was even talk at this time of forming a new political party, which would be made up of people who disagreed with both the Labour and Conservative party policies. In 1981, the Social-Democratic Liberal Alliance was created when moderate members of the Labour party joined with members of the Liberal party. The Alliance works together in Parliament, though each party has its own candidate during an election.

Throughout all the criticism, Margaret Thatcher seemed almost to ignore those who were against her and continued following her plan. To show her faith in what she was doing, she did not accept an £11,000 (about $22,000) increase in her salary in 1980. This action didn't stop the complaints, though.

In the middle of her political troubles, Margaret Thatcher and her family did have some lighter moments. While she was redecorating the Ten Downing Street house, she brought in paintings by famous artists and borrowed elegant furniture from the Victoria and Albert Museum in London. The silver the family used on formal occasions was a permanent loan from her old friend Lord Bruntisfield of Belton House near Grantham; Margaret had run errands for him when she was only ten years old.

Margaret Thatcher didn't have much time to relax in her early days in office. Occasionally, though, she and the family could spend a few days at Chequers. Every prime minister has the good fortune to use this country home, which was given for the use of all future prime ministers by Lord Lee of Fareham in 1918. The British armed forces provide the working staff, freeing the prime minister and his or her family from domestic worries. Like the American Camp David, at Chequers the prime minister and family can retreat from the public to quiet and protective surroundings.

Here Margaret Thatcher could entertain political guests and relax as much as she was able. A reporter once asked her how she handled the stress and strain of being prime minister. Thatcher answered, "I've no idea, it's just that I'm a round peg in a square hole. I don't feel any sign of physical strain at all. I've always led an onerous [heavy] timetable, but I like it. I have a tremendous amount of energy, and for the first time in my life it is fully used."

On Christmas and other holidays, Margaret Thatcher rounded up those without families and invited them to be a part of her family at Che-

Margaret and Denis walk through the grounds of Chequers.

quers. Until the death of her stepmother in December 1988, Margaret invited her to come every Christmas, but the second Mrs. Roberts was unable to accept because of family reunions with her own children.

After a short rest at Chequers during that first year in office, Thatcher was ready to go back to Parliament and face the divisions in her own government. Many of her critics claimed that the economic committee she formed at this time was just a way to avoid having her ideas and policies challenged by opponents.

The E Committee, as it was called, was formed

to avoid arguments with cabinet members who disagreed with Thatcher and to promote her new economic policies. She ignored the "wets" and went
her own way with her "dry" supporters. Since this
move caused resentment within the cabinet and the
whole Conservative party, it was a very unhappy
group that met for the annual conference in Blackpool in 1981.

To their charges, she answered, "I will not
change just to court popularity...If ever Conservative government starts to do what it knows is
wrong because it is afraid to do what is right, that
is the time for the Tories to cry 'Stop.' But you
will never need to do that while I am prime
minister."

By the end of her speech, the anger that had
been building within the government cabinet had
been replaced by a new optimism. Party members
gave their new prime minister a six-minute standing ovation.

Chapter/Nine

From Crisis to Crisis: The Falklands

That six-minute standing ovation at Blackpool faded all too quickly. Thatcher returned to a variety of problems—political and personal—in London. Her son, Mark, who had always loved cars and racing, had entered a famous and dangerous car rally, which led from Paris, France, to Dakar, Senegal, in West Africa. The rugged journey across the Sahara Desert was a challenge to any driver.

Margaret Thatcher worried about her son's car racing, and she was always nervous if she knew the exact time he would be driving. For that reason, he did not tell her his schedule in advance. Also, the Thatcher family had an agreement to stay away from major events where another family member might be appearing. At her request, no Thatcher had watched Margaret in the House of Commons because of the nervousness she knew she would experience. So, in January 1982, while Mark Thatcher and a companion were following the route of the rally through Europe and across the desert of North Africa, Margaret Thatcher stayed busy in England and hoped for news from her son when the race was finished.

A British newspaper reporter called Ten Downing Street midway through the race, trying to establish the truth about a rumor that Mark Thatcher was lost in the Sahara Desert after missing a checkpoint along the route. When Carol told her parents about the call, Denis reminded them all that they shouldn't be alarmed because it was just a rumor. They were all relieved when they received news two days later that Mark had been found.

Their relief turned to fear, however, when official communication later brought news that Mark had not been found and was lost somewhere in the Sahara. When the truth was finally told to Margaret, she was caught in a whirlwind of emotion. Despite her personal crisis, she still had to continue her schedule as prime minister. "I had to call a cabinet meeting," she recalls. "I sent down a note that said, 'Please do not mention anything to me.' They didn't." But as she approached the Imperial

Hotel in Bloomsbury one day to address a luncheon meeting, a reporter caught her off-guard and asked her about her son.

"I'm sorry there is no news. Naturally, I am very concerned." Suddenly, Margaret sobbed openly. The journalist's question had broken the control she was keeping on her emotions.

To many, this proved that the Iron Lady was human after all. As Margaret Thatcher wept for her son, mothers all over the country wept with her and voiced their sympathy in cards and letters.

When some private friends of the family offered to fly Denis Thatcher to West Africa to help find his son, he accepted. After six days, Denis called his wife. Mark had been found at last, alive and well.

For Margaret Thatcher, no political problem could have been worse than losing her own son. She has always been very protective of both her children, and even though they are now both adults, she worries about them. Mark moved in 1984 to Dallas, Texas, to become an automobile representative and to start an investment company. Three years later, he married a young woman from Texas, where the couple now lives.

After her son was found, Thatcher again directed all her energies toward the details of her political office. In April 1982, the prime minister faced the greatest political and professional challenge of her first term—the Falklands.

Three hundred miles off the coast of Argentina in South America lies a group of 202 islands called the Falkland Islands. For 150 years they have belonged to Great Britain, although they are located 8,000 miles from the shores of the British Isles. Most of the 1,800 people who live in the Falklands are British, and sheep farming is the major industry. At one time the British government had considered giving the Falkland Islands independence, but the British residents did not want to be separated from their mother country.

Argentina's Leopold Galtieri, however, saw in the Falklands a perfect opportunity to increase his political popularity in his own country. Galtieri thought that by attacking the Falklands and making them part of Argentina, as they had been in the past, he would stand a good chance of winning his country's upcoming presidential election. He believed that the female prime minister of Great Britain would not challenge him because of his country's military strength, as well as the great distance separating the Falklands and England.

General Galtieri underestimated Margaret Thatcher. On March 31, 1982, she was told that

Argentinian ships were on their way to the Falklands. Although some of her most trusted advisers were away, the prime minister called a meeting of the Foreign Office and Ministry of Defense to decide what to do.

Thatcher also contacted U.S. President Ronald Reagan and Secretary of State Alexander Haig for their support and advice. Haig sent his special envoy, Vernon Walters, to reason with General Galtieri. The Argentinian general reportedly said, "The British won't fight." Galtieri went ahead with his plans to attack.

Secretary Haig visited Prime Minister Thatcher at Ten Downing Street to discuss the Falklands issue. After speaking with her, he commented, "She is very tough. I wish we had more like her."

Knowing that the Argentinian fleet would reach the Falklands in forty-eight hours, the British cabinet was in an uproar. For the first time in twenty-five years, an emergency debate was called in the House of Commons on a Saturday morning. A large majority of the members opposed fighting for the islands, but Margaret Thatcher was not going to allow Argentina to take advantage of her or her country.

After an angry exchange of words with the opposition, Thatcher said, "They [the Falkland

Islands residents] are few in number, but they have
the right to live in peace, to choose their own way
of life, and to determine their own allegiance....
Gentlemen, we shall have to fight," she concluded.
Foreign Secretary Lord Carrington resigned in protest, much to the prime minister's disappointment,
and Francis Pym took his place.

The war cabinet met and arranged for a task
force to send two British aircraft carriers and many
other small ships on the long ocean journey to defend the Falklands. Prime Minister Thatcher tried
to negotiate with the Argentinian leader to avoid
war, but he rejected her ideas.

Galtieri ordered his troops to land on the
main island, where they took control of the local
population. Caught in the middle of a bitter winter, the people were helpless without weapons. Galtieri also sent an Argentinian cruiser and two de-
stroyers to attack the approaching British ships,
but a British submarine sank the cruiser. In response, an enemy fighter plane bombed and sank
the British ship HMS *Sheffield*.

Prince Andrew, one of the queen's sons, was a
helicopter pilot on one of the aircraft carriers sent
to the Falkland Islands. As the casualties mounted
on both sides, Queen Elizabeth II and Margaret
Thatcher drew closer together. Having nearly lost

*Soldiers in the Scots guards, a part of the British military forces, board
the* Queen Elizabeth II. *The cruise ship was used as a troop carrier
during the Falklands crisis.*

her own son a few months earlier, Thatcher could understand the feelings of the queen, who was worried about her son's safety.

Margaret Thatcher became completely involved in the Falklands crisis. She could think of nothing but the number of lives being lost in the war. Her friend and adviser, William Whitelaw, warned her not to be overwhelmed by the number of deaths, and not to let emotion sway her at a time like this; she must continue to be a strong leader. With fourteen ships damaged and more than 250 lives lost, Thatcher found this advice difficult to accept, but she managed to hide most of those feelings from the public. As she had said to journalist Kennith Harris earlier in her term, "I was brought up to control your emotions, never talk about yourself, and show your compassion by doing something."

Only Denis and Carol, who stayed by her side during many sleepless nights, saw the depth of her emotion and concern. Denis was a constant help and comforted her by saying, "Don't let it get on top of you, love."

Margaret Thatcher was again a winner when the Argentinians surrendered on June 14, 1982. It was a landmark day for war-weary Britons. At 9:00 P.M., a message came over the wire: "The

A relieved mother greets her son after his safe return from the Falkland Islands.

Falkland Islands are once more under the government desired by their inhabitants." Prime Minister Thatcher heard the news, closed her eyes, and thought, "Rejoice." Later she said, "I felt colossal relief. It was the most marvelous release I have ever had when the news came in. It was a day I dreamed of and lived for. And when the surrender was confirmed...then I knew that whatever the problems I would have in the rest of my period in office, they were as nothing then and now."

The people of Great Britain rejoiced with Margaret Thatcher. Whatever unhappiness they may have felt about their leader before the Falklands conflict was lost in the pride of victory. And that is what many say Thatcher restored to the nation—a sense of pride. The British had lost it after World War II, and now she had found it for them. She had also shown the world that to stand up for one's principles was a matter of honor.

"After the Falklands was over and people outside were cheering," Thatcher recalled, "I went upstairs to the sitting room and just flopped. I felt relief there weren't any more men to be killed or days to carry on."

Chapter/Ten

Making Political History

The Falklands war may have been small, but it gave the world a new view of Britain's prime minister. Her forcefulness gained great respect from international leaders, who had watched her from the sidelines. Realizing she could use power effectively, whether with words or with weapons, they did not wish to test the Iron Lady.

The October Conservative party conference in Brighton came soon after the Falklands victory, and Margaret Thatcher was once again the center of attention. In the eyes of her supporters, she could do no wrong. Although she barely mentioned the Falklands, she gave an impressive political speech that won her another long, loud standing ovation. She remained the party's hero.

Thatcher spoke at the United Nations in June 1982, shortly after the Falklands crisis, where she gained the respect of other world leaders.

In January 1983, Denis and Margaret Thatcher flew to the Falklands together to celebrate the 150th anniversary of British rule. The outpouring of affection for the woman who had stood by them under military attack was unbelievable; the people adored her. She visited the main island and relived the agony of war the Falkland Islands residents had suffered during those four months.

When the Thatchers returned home, however, the mood was quite different. British oil prices were falling, bank interest rates were up, unemployment was rising, and taxes on items such as televisions, cigarettes, and liquor were still increasing.

People complained bitterly over Thatcher's policies, saying she hadn't lived up to her promises. This attitude was not good for business or for the image of the Tory party. Not wanting to drag out the bad feelings in the country any longer, Thatcher finally asked the queen to dissolve Parliament and call for a general election in June 1983.

Labour party leaders prepared themselves to fight a hard campaign against Thatcher, feeling that they had an opportunity to win control of the government. They attacked her record on unemployment, bank rates, and taxes—all the things she had promised in her campaign to improve, but that she hadn't yet been able to change.

As if the critics from the opposition weren't enough, members of her own party cabinet claimed that she was too "headmistressy" or too "bossy." Her reply was, "I have known some very good headmistresses who have launched their pupils on wonderful careers. I had one such myself. I am what I am. Yes, I do believe in trying to persuade people that the things I believe in are the things they should follow....I am far too old to change now."

When the Labour party began criticizing her personality and condemning her decision to enter Falklands conflict, it turned out to be a mistake.

These personal attacks against Thatcher came from
all political sides, and the public showed their response to such campaign tactics. They were dis-
gusted by both the Labour party and the Conservatives who had turned against Thatcher, and came
to her defense by electing her to a second term of
office in June 1983.

In the early days of her second term, Thatcher
reorganized her cabinet. Having never hesitated to
fire friend or foe in the interest of her administra-
tion and of her country, she dismissed Francis
Pym, foreign secretary, and replaced him with Geof-
frey Howe. Pym had dared to disagree with her in
public, which she felt was disloyal.

Loyalty was a quality she had been taught by
her father, and it was one she prized in herself and
others. Years later, in November 1988, she visited
the United States to meet with her friend and ally,
President Ronald Reagan, whose term in office was
coming to an end. She was asked whether she
thought president-elect George Bush's dedication
and loyalty to Reagan were flaws in his character.

With a flash in her blue eyes and an edge to
her voice, she replied, "Look, loyalty to principles,
country, family, and even newspapers is a positive
quality. George Bush has it in abundance and he
has a right to expect it in abundance."

Loyalty to Thatcher from the British people was severely tested in 1984. Arthur Scargill, president of the National Union of Mineworkers, started a personal war against Margaret Thatcher that lasted from March 1984 to March 1985. As she tried to limit the power of trade unions, Scargill planned to force his mineworkers to strike and bring the country to a standstill. His plan didn't work, however, because many of the mineworkers refused to strike.

Defying threats of violence, Thatcher simply closed the mines that weren't needed anymore. Though it was a bitter defeat for Scargill, many Britons also saw it as a major defeat for the trade unions. It wasn't a complete victory for the government, either, because it spent more than £3 billion trying to break the strike.

The queen herself was upset by the year-long strike and publicly disagreed with Thatcher's policy toward the mineworkers, calling it "insensitive." The relationship between these two women was tested by this royal interference in politics.

In the midst of her troubles with the mineworkers, Thatcher's life was threatened while attending the Conservative party conference in Brighton in 1984. At 3:00 P.M., a bomb ripped through five stories of the Grand Hotel where she and

Denis were staying. Members of the Irish Republican Army (IRA), who oppose British rule in Northern Ireland, were blamed for the bomb meant for Thatcher and other members of her government. She had been working late on a speech and had stepped into the washroom; this probably saved her life.

After the narrow escape, Thatcher told reporters her attitude toward life had changed. "Life is infinitely more precious to me now. When something like that happens, it alters your perspective. You're not going to be worried or complain about silly things anymore, but you try to do the right thing about the big things. And you must go right on doing the right thing."

Carol, Mark, and Denis were visibly shocked by the attack against Margaret. They all became even more protective of her than they had been in the past. Shortly after this incident, Mark was walking behind his mother when a stranger approached. He moved quickly to her side, ready to protect her from harm. The family still refused, however, to become more visible in Margaret Thatcher's political life, maintaining that it was important to keep their home life and public life as separate as possible.

Although brave and courageous in her words

Rooms in the middle section of the Grand Hotel were destroyed by a bomb meant for Prime Minister Thatcher and her cabinet.

Thatcher and former U.S. President Ronald Reagan.

to the public, as she has been throughout every personal crisis in her life, Margaret Thatcher was shaken. Her stand against terrorism, always firm, became tougher than it had been in the past. This incident may have influenced her decision to support President Reagan in his bombing raids against Libya. The United States had asked to use British territory while planning and carrying out these raids on the north African country whose leader, Muammar Qadhafi, was thought to be responsible for many terrorist actions around the world.

Thatcher also felt she owed the United States government a favor for its support during the Falklands crisis. But the British public, her own Conservative party, and the Labour party were all angry with her for allowing the Americans to use British soil. Although they protested against it, both in Parliament and in the streets of London, Thatcher stuck by her decision.

The middle years of Thatcher's second term were marked by internal fighting within her cabinet, bankruptcies across the country, and takeovers of British companies by American industries. This last problem upset the British people the most. The public and some members of Parliament were afraid of losing control of their own country to Americans and other foreign powers.

Public opinion was turning against Margaret Thatcher. She felt she needed something to make the people of Great Britain believe in her again. She found it in March 1987—a trip to Russia. The prime minister was invited to Moscow to meet with the Soviet Union's daring and progressive new new leader, Mikhail Gorbachev. Soviet leaders were eager to impress Thatcher, whom they still saw as the Iron Lady. As for Thatcher herself, she was impressed with Mikhail Gorbachev; he seemed to be her kind of leader. His desire to change his country's centrally controlled economy by giving people a chance to work for themselves was very

The prime minister and Mikhail Gorbachev during Thatcher's 1987 visit to the USSR.

similar to her own philosophy.

The two leaders appeared to respect and like each other, and after thirteen hours of private talks, Thatcher was allowed to appear for fifty minutes on Soviet television. In a country where opposing political views are not encouraged, this was a real breakthrough. Thatcher answered a variety of questions, such as what she ate for breakfast and whether it was true that she liked work better than anything else. She replied, "Frankly, work is more interesting than anything else." She also quoted from Noel Coward, a British playwright: "...work is more fun than fun."

Thatcher was careful to balance her enthusiasm for the new Soviet leader with a healthy suspicion of him and his plans for reform. "As long as the West stands up for freedom in the battle of ideas," Thatcher said in 1988, "the world will be safer. Mikhail Gorbachev has vision, boldness, and courage. In my dealings with him, he has done what he has undertaken."

The visit to the Soviet Union restored the public's faith in Thatcher's abilities as a world leader. Feeling she needed to take advantage of the public goodwill, Thatcher set an election date in an attempt to win a third term for her Conservative government. She chose June 11, 1987.

The Labour party was desperate to defeat the woman who seemed to be on her way to a third election victory. In a frustrated attempt to stop her, they attacked her weaknesses as a woman. Neil Kinnock, the Welsh Labour leader, claimed Thatcher was hard, unfeeling, and heartless. British voters rebelled against this kind of attack, as well as Labour's plans to cut the defense budget.

The race was close. For a time, no one knew whether Margaret Thatcher or Neil Kinnock would lead Great Britain. Yet on June 11, Thatcher won a historic, but slender, victory as prime minister for a third term.

    She won mainly because the majority of the
voters thought she had accomplished what she said
she would achieve: greater numbers of the British
people owned their own homes, and Britain was
once again becoming a prosperous and powerful
nation. Unless the Labour party offers the British
people a more dynamic leader or a more persua-
sive set of policies, Margaret Thatcher may stay in
power for years to come.

    However, the danger of power is its misuse,
something Thatcher has been accused of by her
critics. The effects of the year-long miners strike in
1984 and Thatcher's anti-union policies can still be
seen today in northern England, where the majority of the nation's 2 million unemployed live. She
has been accused of helping only the middle class
and neglecting the welfare and concerns of the
working and lower classes. In addition, her decision to cut welfare to those under eighteen years
old was seen by some to be a cruel act.

    In Great Britain, most students graduate from
school when they are sixteen years old. Before
1987, sixteen-year-olds could register for unemployment benefits, which helped pay for food, clothing,
and shelter until they were able to find a job. In
northern England, where the unemployment rate
has been very high, people felt this program was

especially helpful. Margaret Thatcher, though, believed that welfare was costing the government too much money, so she eliminated benefits to people under eighteen years of age. This has led to problems in a country where one out of nine people under the age of twenty-five is unemployed.

Teenagers who can no longer rely on money from the government have begun moving into the larger cities in search of jobs. But with no money and no place to live, they often have to sleep in subway stations or abandoned buildings. Great Britain is not alone in facing the problems of homeless people, however, as more and more countries are trying to find a solution.

Thatcher's solution in the past decade has been to create a youth training plan to assist unemployed and unskilled teenagers. In this program, the government and employer share the costs of providing a trainee with a place to live and a salary while he or she learns a new skill. Such policies reflect Thatcher's belief in self-help rather than government support. Her attitude, which comes from her father's teachings and her own experience, is best expressed in the last line of her favorite saying from Abraham Lincoln: "You cannot help men permanently by doing for them what they could and should do for themselves."

Added to the continuing unemployment problems was the exposure in 1986 of the secrets of the British spy system in a book called *Spycatcher*, whose publication Margaret Thatcher tried unsuccessfully to stop. When the author moved to Australia and wrote the book, he was no longer violating the Official Secrets Act, which he would have done as a resident of England. Because of this, Thatcher was unable to ban the book. But she brought more publicity to it by her anger than it might have otherwise received.

Also, in 1988, Thatcher threatened the rights of the free press by banning broadcast interviews with Irish extremists. She refused to give terrorists a platform from which to speak, either through the printed word or through free time on television. To show it was serious, the government fined a London journalist $37,000 for defying the ban and for not revealing his sources for an article. The International Press Institute protested against the government's interference with freedom of the press.

Unlike the United States, Great Britain has neither a written constitution nor a bill of rights, making these democratic freedoms difficult to defend. The "constitution" of Great Britain is composed of many different written documents, such as the Magna Carta (written in 1215), as well as many unwritten parts that have been developed throughout the years according to British tradition and customs. Both Parliament and the people have the power to change part of the constitution at any time. Under this system of government, the press can only challenge parliamentary restrictions by appealing to the High Court in London or to the European Commission on Human Rights.

In spite of her sometimes poor relationship with the press, Margaret Thatcher's views against socialism and for private ownership have made her "the most famous woman in the world" and assured her place in history as a great prime minister. Some have even compared her leadership to that of Winston Churchill.

But what of the future of Thatcher and Thatcherism?

In her personal life, Thatcher has shown that politics and family can go together. Although the freedom and privacy of her family life has suffered because of her career, she still maintains that "family are always your closest friends."

Politically, Thatcher has proven to be a success. At sixty-four, she continues to dominate both her party and her country. With a record surplus of £10 billion in her 1988 budget, and a growing, successful economy, she hopes to reform the

British educational system, to lessen spending in the National Health Service, and to make her policies and philosophies a way of life for Britain. Her greatest challenge is to carry out these ambitious plans and also to reunite her divided country.

Although labeled a Conservative, Thatcher has never been known to follow the party without question. In her personal experience, she has rebelled against the standard role reserved for women, from entering politics in the early 1940s to becoming the first female prime minister in Great Britain's history. Margaret Thatcher has always lived by the advice her father gave her many years ago: "Margaret, never do things just because other people do them. Make up your own mind about what you are going to do and persuade people to go your way." Whether the British people have supported or approved her actions as prime minister, almost all agree she has set and firmly followed her own course.

Italians call her "Mama Thatcher—strong leader, strong leader."

In time, history may echo that same sentiment.

Selected Bibliography

"Academe Snubs Thatcher." *Christian Century* (March 6, 1985): 35.

Allen, Jim. *The Grantham Connection.* Grantham: Grantham Book Center, 1986.

Baum, Julian. "Britain's Thatcher Unchallenged." *Christian Science Monitor* (January 3, 1988): 6.

Berss, Marcia, and Forbes, Malcolm S., Jr. "I Envy President Reagan." *Forbes* (July 28, 1986): 16.

Bishop, James. "Why I Want a Third Term." *Illustrated London News* (June 1987): 16.

"Brighton's Solid Citizens." *The Economist* (October 12, 1988): 67.

"Britain's Iron Lady." *Newsweek* (May 14, 1979): 20.

Goodwin, J. "Tea With Margaret Thatcher." *Ladies Home Journal* (November 1987): 135.

Grantham Journal. May 23, 1952; November 29, 1985. Grantham, England.

Greer, Germaine. "Thatcher." *Lear's* (May/June 1988): 86.

Harris, Kenneth. *Thatcher*. London: Little, Brown & Co., 1988.

———. Interview on C-Span, December 16, 1988.

"The Iron Lady Stands Alone." *Time* (April 28, 1986): 24.

Jenkins, Peter. *Mrs. Thatcher's Revolution: The Ending of the Socialist Era*. Cambridge: Harvard University Press, 1988.

Junor, Penny. *Margaret Thatcher: Wife, Mother, Politician*. London: Sidgwick & Jackson, 1983.

Keay, Douglas. "Margaret Thatcher's Life Story." *Good Housekeeping* (April 1985): 107.

Kirkland, Richard I. "A Year to Shout About." *Fortune* (January 4, 1988): 34.

———. "What Maggie Has Wrought." *Fortune* (June 8, 1987): 91.

"Margaret Thatcher Opens Up on her Life as a Woman, Mother and World Leader." *People* (August 18, 1988): 28.

"Mark Thatcher Bridles." *People* (March 2, 1987): 26.

Mayer, Alan J. *Madame Prime Minister*. New York: Newsweek Books, 1979.

New York Times. September 15, 1985.

Reed, David. "Maggie Thatcher: She's All Backbone." *Reader's Digest* (November 1987): 213.

Selbourne, D. "Life With Maggie." *Harper's*. (September 1985): 73.

Stoppard, Dr. Miriam, Television interview with Margaret Thatcher. *Woman to Woman*, London, England. 1986.

Thatcher, Margaret. Speech given to Kesteven and Grantham Girls' School, Grantham, England, February 12, 1982.

"The Thatcher Revolution." *National Review* (November 20, 1987): 20.

"Thatcher Takes on the Welfare State." *U.S. News and World Report* (June 17, 1985): 12.

"Thatcher's Self-Help Revolution." *U.S. News and World Report* (May 9, 1988): 38.

"3,164 Days and Counting." *Time* (January 11, 1988): 53.

"A Tory Wind of Change." *Time* (May 14, 1979): 30.

Toynbee, Polly. "Is Margaret Thatcher a Woman?" *Washington Monthly* (May 1988): 34.

"What Maggie Hath Wrought." *U.S. News and World Report* (April 6, 1987): 30.

Whitaker, Mark, Clifton, Tony, and Foote, Donna. "Thatcher's Two Britains." *Newsweek* (June 22, 1987): 28.

Wickstead, Margaret Goodrich. "Personality of the Month." *Lincolnshire Life* (April 1982).

Wilson, Andrew B. "A Talk With Thatcher: It Takes a Long Time to Turn the Economy Around." *Business Week* (February 25, 1985): 42.

Woollcott, Raymond. Conversation with the author in Dartford, England. December 1988.

Index

illness of, 70; influence on Margaret of, 7, 8, 56; Margaret's marriage and, 49; marriage of, 8; as mayor, 21; politics and, 21-22, 46; religious views of, 11, 13, 15, 17; welfare and, 16

Roberts, Beatrice (mother), 8, 11, 13, 20, 23, 67

Roberts, Margaret Hilda. *See* Thatcher, Margaret

Roberts, Muriel (sister), 11, 20, 25

Scargill, Arthur, 127

Social-Democratic Liberal Alliance, 109

socialism, 90

Spycatcher, 136

Ten Downing Street, 100, 102, 103, 109, 114, 117

Thames River, 57

Thatcher, Carol (daughter), 52, 64, 85, 97, 101, 102, 114, 128

Thatcher, Denis (husband): business of, 69; courtship of Margaret and, 45, 47, 49; family of, 47, 48, 49; as a father, 115; as a husband, 51, 54, 73, 88, 94, 101, 120; marriage of, 50-51; the news media and, 86; previous marriage of, 50, 79; retirement of, 83-84

Thatcher, Margaret: Alfred Roberts and, 7, 8, 15, 71, 100, 126; assassination attempt on, 127, 128; as a barrister, 52, 54, 56; birth of, 6, 11; as a Conservative, 34, 39, 40, 138; as Conservative party leader, 6, 77, 79, 81, 83, 84, 85, 86, 91, 96; early education of, 17, 18, 21, 22, 24, 26; in the Falkland Islands, 124;

foreign relations and, 84-85, 91, 92, 94, 108; home life of, 105, 109, 128, 137; as the Iron Lady, 91-92, 115, 123, 131; marriage of, 6, 51-52; as a member of Parliament, 56, 57, 61, 62, 63-64, 66, 67, 68, 69, 70, 71, 74; mineworkers' strike and, 127, 134; as a mother, 52, 54, 55, 56, 63, 64, 85, 86, 113, 114, 115; the news media and, 62-63, 72, 73, 136, 137; Oxford Graduate Association and, 39, 40; Oxford University and Somerville College, 26, 27-28, 29, 30, 31, 32, 33, 34, 35, 36, 37, 38, 51; party conferences and, 86-87, 88, 89, 95, 112, 123; policies of, 71, 72-73, 90, 94, 95, 134, 135, 137; political campaigns of, 40, 41, 42-44, 46, 47, 48, 49, 55-56, 76, 97, 98, 125, 133; as prime minister, 7, 100, 101, 104, 105-107, 109-112, 116, 123, 125, 126, 130, 133, 134, 136, 137, 138; public image of, 76, 83, 92, 95, 98; religion and, 13, 15; in Russia, 131-133; at The Temple, 51, 52; terrorism and, 130, 136; as a wife, 51, 63, 69, 83

Thatcher, Mark (son), 52, 64, 86, 101, 102, 113, 114, 115, 128

Thatcherism, 90, 137

Tory party. *See* Conservative party

Wickstead, Margaret Goodrich, 31, 34

Wilson, Harold, 69, 70, 74, 91, 92

Woollcott, Raymond, 44, 46, 47

World War II, 10, 11, 21, 22, 122

Worth, George, 37